STUDY NOTES

COMPUTER APTITUDE

For All Banking Exams

COMPUTER APTITUDE

COMPUTER FUNDAMENTALS TUTORIAL

Computer fundamentals tutorial provides basic and advanced concepts of Bootstrap. Our Computer fundamentals is designed for beginners and professionals.

Computer is an electronic device i.e. used to work with information or compute. It is derived from the Latin word "computare" which means to calculate.

Our Computer fundamentals tutorial includes all topics of Computer fundamentals such as input devices, output devices, memory, CPU, motherboard, computer network, virus, software, hardware etc.

What is Computer?

A computer is a programmable electronic device that accepts raw data as input and processes it with a set of instructions (a program) to produce the result as output. It renders output just after performing mathematical and logical operations and can save the output for future use. It can process numerical as well as non-numerical calculations. The term "computer" is derived from the Latin word "computare" which means to calculate.

A computer is designed to execute applications and provides a variety of solutions through integrated hardware and software components. It works with the help of programs and represents the decimal numbers through a string of binary digits. It also has a memory that stores the data, programs, and result of processing. The components of a computer such as machinery that includes wires, transistors, circuits, hard disk are called hardware. Whereas, the programs and data are called software.

It is believed that the Analytical Engine was the first computer which was invented by Charles Babbage in 1837. It used punch cards as read-only memory. Charles Babbage is also known as the father of the computer.

The basic parts without which a computer cannot work are as follows:

- **Processor:** It executes instructions from software and hardware.
- **Memory:** It is the primary memory for data transfer between the CPU and storage.

- **Motherboard:** It is the part that connects all other parts or components of a computer.
- **Storage Device:** It permanently stores the data, e.g., hard drive.
- **Input Device:** It allows you to communicate with the computer or to input data, e.g., a keyboard.
- **Output Device:** It enables you to see the output, e.g., monitor.

Computers are divided into different types based on different criteria. Based on the size, a computer can be divided into five types:

1. Micro Computer
2. Mini Computer
3. Mainframe Computer
4. Super Computer
5. Workstations

1. Micro Computer:

It is a single-user computer which has less speed and storage capacity than the other types. It uses a microprocessor as a CPU. The first microcomputer was built with 8-bit microprocessor chips. The common examples of microcomputers include laptops, desktop computers, personal digital assistant (PDA), tablets, and smartphones. Microcomputers are generally designed and developed for general usage like browsing, searching for information, internet, MS Office, social media, etc.

2. Mini Computer:

Mini-computers are also known as "Midrange Computers." They are not designed for a single. They are multi-user computers designed to support multiple users simultaneously. So, they are generally used by small businesses and firms. Individual departments of a company use these computers for specific purposes. For example, the admission department of a University can use a Mini-computer for monitoring the admission process.

3. Mainframe Computer:

It is also a multi-user computer capable of supporting thousands of users simultaneously. They are used by large firms and government organizations to run their business operations as they can store and process large amounts of data. For example, Banks, universities, and insurance companies use mainframe computers to store the data of their customers, students, and policyholders, respectively.

4. Super Computer:

Super-computers are the fastest and most expensive computers among all types of computers. They have huge storage capacities and computing speeds and thus can perform millions of instructions per second. The super-computers are task-specific and thus used for specialized applications such as large-scale numerical problems in scientific and engineering disciplines including applications in electronics, petroleum engineering, weather forecasting, medicine, space research and more. For example, NASA uses supercomputers for launching space satellites and monitoring and controlling them for space exploration.

5. Work stations:

It is a single-user computer. Although it is like a personal computer, it has a more powerful microprocessor and a higher-quality monitor than a microcomputer. In terms of storage capacity and speed, it comes between a personal computer and minicomputer. Work stations are generally used for specialized applications such as desktop publishing, software development, and engineering designs.

Benefits of Using a Computer:

- **Increases your productivity:** A computer increases your productivity. For example, after having a basic understanding of a word processor, you can create, edit, store, and print the documents easily and quickly.
- **Connects to the Internet:** It connects you to the internet that allows you to send emails, browse content, gain information, use social media platforms, and more. By connecting to the internet, you can also connect to your long-distance friends and family members.

- **Storage:** A computer allows you to store a large amount of information, e.g., you can store your projects, ebooks, documents, movies, pictures, songs, and more.
- **Organized Data and Information:** It not only allows you to store data but also enables you to organize your data. For example, you can create different folders to store different data and information and thus can search for information easily and quickly.
- **Improves your abilities:** It helps write good English if you are not good at spelling and grammar. Similarly, if you are not good at math, and don't have a great memory, you can use a computer to perform calculations and store the results.
- **Assist the physically challenged:** It can be used to help the physically challenged, e.g., Stephen Hawking, who was not able to speak used computer to speak. It also can be used to help blind people by installing special software to read what is on the screen.
- **Keeps you entertained:** You can use the computer to listen to songs, watch movies, play games and more.

The computer has become a part of our life. There are plenty of things that we do in a day are dependent on a computer. Some of the common examples are as follows:

1. **ATM:** While withdrawing cash from an ATM, you are using a computer that enables the ATM to take instructions and dispense cash accordingly.
2. **Digital currency:** A computer keeps a record of your transactions and balance in your account and the money deposited in your account in a bank is stored as a digital record or digital currency.
3. **Trading:** Stock markets use computers for day to day trading. There are many advanced algorithms based on computers that handle trading without involving humans.
4. **Smartphone:** The smartphone that we use throughout the day for calling, texting, browsing is itself a computer.
5. **VoIP:** All voice over IP communication (VoIP) is handled and done by computers.

HISTORY OF COMPUTERS

The first counting device was used by the primitive people. They used sticks, stones and bones as counting tools. As human mind and technology improved with time more computing devices were developed. Some of the popular computing devices starting with the first to recent ones are described below;

Generations of Computers

A generation of computers refers to the specific improvements in computer technology with time. In 1946, electronic pathways called circuits were developed to perform the counting. It replaced the gears and other mechanical parts used for counting in previous computing machines.

In each new generation, the circuits became smaller and more advanced than the previous generation circuits. The miniaturization helped increase the speed, memory and power of computers. There are five generations of computers which are described below;

First Generation Computers

The first generation (1946-1959) computers were slow, huge and expensive. In these computers, vacuum tubes were used as the basic components of CPU and memory. These computers were mainly depended on batch operating system and punch cards. Magnetic tape and paper tape were used as output and input devices in this generation;

Some of the popular first generation computers are;

- **ENIAC** (Electronic Numerical Integrator and Computer)
- **EDVAC** (Electronic Discrete Variable Automatic Computer)
- **UNIVACI**(Universal Automatic Computer)
- **IBM-701**
- **IBM-650**

Second Generation Computers

The second generation (1959-1965) was the era of the transistor computers. These computers used transistors which were cheap, compact and consuming less power; it made transistor computers faster than the first generation computers.

In this generation, magnetic cores were used as the primary memory and magnetic disc and tapes were used as the secondary storage. Assembly language and programming languages like COBOL and FORTRAN, and Batch processing and multiprogramming operating systems were used in these computers.

Some of the popular second generation computers are;

- IBM 1620
- IBM 7094
- CDC 1604
- CDC 3600
- UNIVAC 1108

Third Generation Computers

The third generation computers used integrated circuits (ICs) instead of transistors. A single IC can pack huge number of transistors which increased the power of a computer and reduced the cost. The computers also became more reliable, efficient and smaller in size. These generation computers used remote processing, time-sharing, multi programming as operating system. Also, the high-level programming languages like FORTRON-II TO IV, COBOL, PASCAL PL/1, ALGOL-68 were used in this generation.

Some of the popular third generation computers are;

- IBM-360 series
- Honeywell-6000 series
- PDP(Personal Data Processor)
- IBM-370/168

- TDC-316

Fourth Generation Computers

The fourth generation (1971-1980) computers used very large scale integrated (VLSI) circuits; a chip containing millions of transistors and other circuit elements. These chips made this generation computers more compact, powerful, fast and affordable. These generation computers used real time, time sharing and distributed operating system. The programming languages like C, C++, DBASE were also used in this generation.

Some of the popular fourth generation computers are;

- DEC 10
- STAR 1000
- PDP 11
- CRAY-1(Super Computer)
- CRAY-X-MP(Super Computer)

Fifth Generation Computers

In fifth generation (1980-till date) computers, the VLSI technology was replaced with ULSI (Ultra Large Scale Integration). It made possible the production of microprocessor chips with ten million electronic components. This generation computers used parallel processing hardware and AI (Artificial Intelligence) software. The programming languages used in this generation were C, C++, Java, .Net, etc.

Some of the popular fifth generation computers are;

- Desktop
- Laptop
- NoteBook
- UltraBook
- ChromeBook

Types of Computer

We can categorize computer in two ways: on the basis of data handling capabilities and size.

On the basis of data handling capabilities, the computer is of three types:

- Analogue Computer
- Digital Computer
- Hybrid Computer

1) Analogue Computer

Analogue computers are designed to **process analogue data**. Analogue data is continuous data that changes continuously and cannot have discrete values. We can say that analogue computers are used where we don't need exact values always such as speed, temperature, pressure and current.

Analogue computers directly accept the data from the measuring device without first converting it into numbers and codes. They measure the continuous changes in physical quantity and generally render output as a reading on a dial or scale. **Speedometer** and **mercury thermometer** are examples of analogue computers.

Advantages of using analogue computers:

- It allows real-time operations and computation at the same time and continuous representation of all data within the rage of the analogue machine.
- In some applications, it allows performing calculations without taking the help of transducers for converting the inputs or outputs to digital electronic form and vice versa.
- The programmer can scale the problem for the dynamic range of the analogue computer. It provides insight into the problem and helps understand the errors and their effects.

Types of analogue computers:

- **Slide Rules**: It is one of the simplest types of **mechanical analogue computers**. It was developed to perform **basic mathematical calculations**. It is made of two rods. To perform the calculation, the hashed rod is slid to line up with the markings on another rod.

- **Differential Analysers**: It was developed to perform **differential calculations**. It performs integration using wheel-and-disc mechanisms to solve differential calculations.
- **Castle Clock**: It was invented by **Al-Jarazi**. It was able to save programming instructions. Its height was around 11 feet and it was provided with the display of time, the zodiac, and the solar and lunar orbits. This device also could allow users to set the length of the day as per the current season.
- **Electronic Analogue Computer**: In this type of analogue computer, electrical signals flow through capacitors and resistors to simulate physical phenomena. Here, the mechanical interaction of components docs not take place. The voltage of the electrical signal generates the appropriate displays.

2) Digital Computer

Digital computer is designed to perform calculations and logical operations at high speed. It accepts the raw data as input in the form of digits or binary numbers (0 and 1) and processes it with programs stored in its memory to produce the output. All modern computers like laptops, desktops including smartphones that we use at home or office are digital computers.

Advantages of digital computers:

- It allows you to store a large amount of information and to retrieve it easily whenever you need it.
- You can easily add new features to digital systems more easily.
- Different applications can be used in digital systems just by changing the program without making any changes in hardware
- The cost of hardware is less due to the advancement in the IC technology.
- It offers high speed as the data is processed digitally.
- It is highly reliable as it uses error correction codes.
- Reproducibility of results is higher as the output is not affected by noise, temperature, humidity, and other properties of its components.

3) Hybrid Computer

Hybrid computer has features of both analogue and digital computer. It is **fast like an analogue** computer and has memory and **accuracy like digital computers**. It can process both continuous and discrete data. It accepts analogue signals and convert them into digital form before processing. So, it is widely used in specialized applications where both analogue and digital data is processed. For example, a processor is used in petrol pumps that converts the measurements of fuel flow into quantity and price. Similarly, they are used in airplanes, hospitals, and scientific applications.

Advantages of using hybrid computers:

- Its computing speed is very high due to the all-parallel configuration of the analogue subsystem.
- It produces precise and quick results that are more accurate and useful.
- It has the ability to solve and manage big equation in real-time.
- It helps in the on-line data processing.

1) Supercomputer

Supercomputers are the **biggest and fastest computers**. They are designed to process huge amount of data. A supercomputer can **process trillions of instructions in a second**. It has thousands of interconnected processors.

Supercomputers are particularly used in **scientific and engineering applications** such as weather forecasting, scientific simulations and nuclear energy research. The first supercomputer was developed by **Roger Cray in 1976**.

Characteristics or applications of supercomputers:

- It has the ability to decrypt your password to enhance protection for security reasons.
- It produces excellent results in animations.
- It is used for virtual testing of nuclear weapons and critical medical tests.
- It can study and understand climate patterns and forecast weather conditions. It can run in NOAA's system (National Oceanic and Atmospheric Administration) that can execute any type of simple and logical data.

- It helps in designing the flight simulators for pilots at the beginner level for their training.
- It helps in extracting useful information from data storage centres or cloud system. For example, in insurance companies.
- It has played a vital role in managing the online currency world such as stock market and bitcoin.
- It helps in the diagnosis of various critical diseases and in producing accurate results in brain injuries, strokes, etc.
- It helps in scientific research areas by accurately analysing data obtained from exploring the solar system, satellites, and movement of Earth.
- It also used in a smog control system where it predicts the level of fog and other pollutants in the atmosphere.

2) Mainframe computer

Mainframe computers are designed to support hundreds or thousands of users simultaneously. They can support multiple programs at the same time. It means they can execute different processes simultaneously. These features of mainframe computers make them ideal for big organizations like banking and telecom sectors, which need to manage and process high volume of data.

Mainframe computers are designed to **support hundreds or thousands of users simultaneously**. They can **support multiple programs** at the same time. It means they can execute different processes simultaneously.

These features of mainframe computers make them ideal for big organizations like banking and telecom sectors, which need to manage and process a high volume of data that requires integer operations such as indexing, comparisons, etc.

Characteristics of Mainframe Computers:

- It can process huge amount of data, e.g. millions of transactions in a second in the banking sector.
- It has a very long life. It can run smoothly for up to 50 years after proper installation.

- It gives excellent performance with large scale memory management.
- It has the ability to share or distribute its workload among other processors and input/output terminals.
- There are fewer chances of error or bugs during processing in mainframe computers. If any error occurs it can fix it quickly without affecting the performance.
- It has the ability to protect the stored data and other ongoing exchange of information and data.

Applications of mainframe computers:

- In **health care,** it enabled hospitals to maintain a record of their millions of patients in order to contact them for treatment or related to their appointment, medicine updates or disease updates.
- In the **field of defence**, it allows the defence departments to share a large amount of sensitive information with other branches of defence.
- In the **field of education**, it helps big universities to store, manage and retrieve data related to their courses, admissions, students, teachers, employees and affiliated schools and colleges.
- In the **retail sector**, the retail companies that have a huge customer base and branches use mainframe computers to handle and execute information related to their inventory management, customer management, and huge transactions in a short duration.

3) Miniframe or Minicomputer

It is a **midsize multiprocessing computer**. It consists of two or more processors and can support **4 to 200 users at one time**. Miniframe computers are used in institutes and departments for tasks such as billing, accounting and inventory management. A minicomputer **lies between the mainframe and microcomputer** as it is smaller than mainframe but larger than a microcomputer.

Characteristics of miniframe or minicomputer:

- It is light weight that makes it easy to carry and fit anywhere.
- It is less expensive than mainframe computers.
- It is very fast compared to its size.

- It remains charged for a long time.
- It does not require a controlled operational environment.

Characteristics of miniframe or minicomputer:

- It is light weight that makes it easy to carry and fit anywhere.
- It is less expensive than mainframe computers.
- It is very fast compared to its size.
- It remains charged for a long time.
- It does not require a controlled operational environment.

Applications of minicomputers:

A minicomputer is mainly used to perform three primary functions, which are as follows:

Process control: It was used for process control in manufacturing. It mainly performs two primary functions that are collecting data and feedback. If any abnormality occurs in the process, it is detected by the minicomputer and necessary adjustments are made accordingly.

Data management: It is an excellent device for small organizations to collect, store and share data. Local hospitals and hotels can use it to maintain the records of their patients and customers respectively.

Communications Portal: It can also play the role of a communication device in larger systems by serving as a portal between a human operator and a central processor or computer.

4) Workstation

Workstation is a **single user computer** that is designed for **technical or scientific applications**. It has a faster microprocessor, a large amount of RAM and high speed graphic adapters. It generally **performs a specific job with great expertise**; accordingly, they are of different types such as graphics workstation, music workstation and engineering design workstation.

Characteristics of workstation computer:

- It is a high-performance computer system designed for a single user for business or professional use.
- It has larger storage capacity, better graphics, and more powerful CPU than a personal computer.
- It can handle animation, data analysis, CAD, audio and video creation and editing.

Any computer that has the following **five features**, can be termed as a workstation or can be used as a workstation.

- **Multiple Processor Cores**: It has more processor cores than simple laptops or computers.
- **ECC RAM**: It is provided with Error-correcting code memory that can fix memory errors before they affect the system's performance.
- **RAID (Redundant Array of Independent Disks)**: It refers to multiple internal hard drives to store or process data. RAID can be of different types, for example, there can be multiple drives to process data or mirrored drives where if one drive does not work than other starts functioning.
- **SSD**: It is better than conventional hard-disk drives. It does not have moving parts, so the chances of physical failure are very less.
- **Optimized, Higher end GPU**: It reduces the load on CPU. E.g., CPU has to do less work while processing the screen output.

5) Microcomputer

Microcomputer is also known as a personal computer. It is a general-purpose computer that is designed for individual use. It has a microprocessor as a central processing unit, memory, storage area, input unit and output unit. Laptops and desktop computers are examples of microcomputers. They are suitable for personal work that may be making an assignment, watching a movie, or at office for office work.

Characteristics of a microcomputer:

- It is the smallest in size among all types of computers.
- A limited number of software can be used.

- It is designed for personal work and applications. Only one user can work at a time.
- It is less expansive and easy to use.
- It does not require the user to have special skills or training to use it.
- Generally, comes with single semiconductor chip.
- It is capable of multitasking such as printing, scanning, browsing, watching videos, etc.

FAQs on the Types of Computers

1. What are the Three Main Types of Computers?

On the basis of data handling capabilities, the three main types of computers are:

- Analog computers
- Digital computers
- Hybrid computers

2. What is a Workstation?

A workstation is a kind of computer that can be used for software development, desktop publishing, and creating engineering applications. Although a modest amount of processing power is present in a workstation, it has relatively good graphical capabilities.

3. What do you Understand by the Term Mainframe?

A mainframe is often very expensive and a very large type of computer. These kinds of computers have the potential to support hundreds and even thousands of people in one go. Furthermore, programs can run simultaneously, and concurrent execution is possible in mainframe computers.

4. What are the advantages of Analog computers?

The advantages of Analog computers are that it represents the data within the system's range and enables users for real-time computations. These as well carry out the calculations without using transducers. Analog systems come in different types, such as Hybrid computers, Digital computers, Castlerock, Electronic Analog computers, slide rules, and differential analyzers. Each of these has advantages and drawbacks of its own. Students who need a thorough explanation of each can go through these on Javatpoint website.

5. What are slide rules?

The simplest analog computer system is the slide. It is used to carry out numerous mathematical computations. These are made up of two rods. The rod slides off with the marking on the other rod when there any calculations are made. In contrast, differential calculations are performed using differential analyzers. These operate using a wheel and disc system. Through Javatpoint, where correct explanations are given that are simple for all pupils to understand, they can learn all the concepts easily.

6. What are digital computers?

All logical operations are completed quickly and efficiently by digital computers. They work with digital or binary numbers. One of the numerous benefits of digital computers is that they can store a large amount of data. Digital computers can simply add new functionality. The cost of these computers is quite low, and the data processing is done at high speed. The cost is quite low, and the data processing is done quickly digitally. For further information about the different sorts of computers, students can consult Javatpoint.

7. What are mainframe computers?

The mainframe is a type of computer that can be characterized as an expensive and substantial computer system. This is very powerful as they have the potential to support numerous users at the same time.

These also facilitate different program executions. It provides great performance with extensive memory management and has a long lifespan. Another advantage of using a mainframe is that errors are often quite infrequent, but when they do occur, the system automatically corrects them. They also have a wide range of applications.

8. What do you understand about Hybrid computers?

Digital and analog computers are combined in order to create hybrid computers. Although the accuracy and memory are close to digital computers, the speed is similar to analogue computers. Before the process, these kinds of computers take the analogue signals and transform them into digital signals. These are typically used in specialist applications that combine analog and digital data. Hybrid computers have the capability to resolve complicated problems in real-time and contain a very high speed.

9. Which type of computer has two or more processors and it supports 4 to 200 users at one time.

A minicomputer is a multiprocessing computer of medium size. This type of computer has two or more CPUs and can accommodate 4 to 200 users in one go.

Computer Components

There are 5 main computer components that are given below:

- Input Devices
- CPU
- Output Devices
- Primary Memory
- Secondary Memory

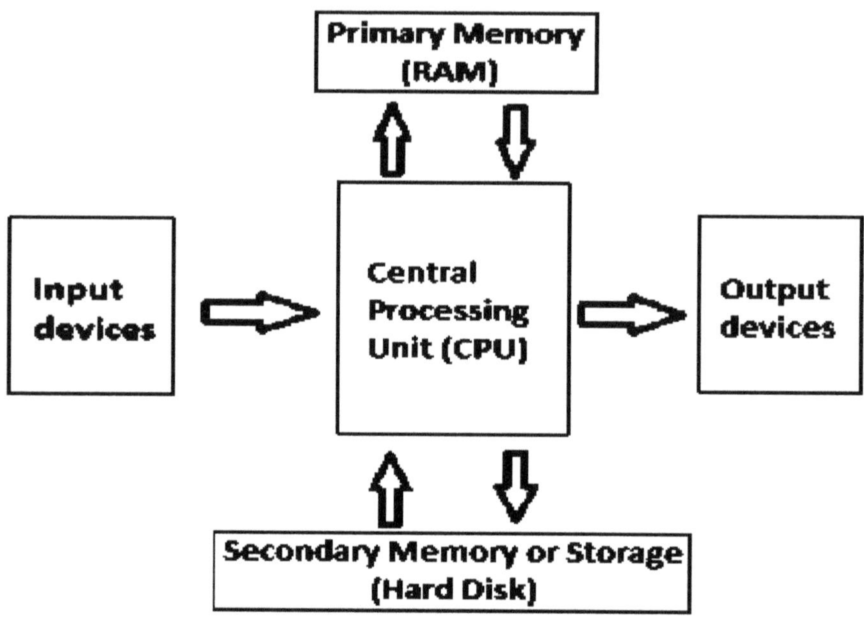

The operations of computer components are given below:

1) Inputting: It is the process of entering raw data, instructions and information into the computer. It is performed with the help of input devices.

2) Storing: The computer has primary memory and secondary storage to store data and instructions. It stores the data before sending it to CPU for processing and also stores the processed data before displaying it as output.

3) Processing: It is the process of converting the raw data into useful information. This process is performed by the CPU of the computer. It takes the raw data from storage, processes it and then sends back the processed data to storage.

4) Outputting: It is the process of presenting the processed data through output devices like monitor, printer and speakers.

5) Controlling: This operation is performed by the control unit that is part of CPU. The control unit ensures that all basic operations are executed in a right manner and sequence.

Input Devices

Input device enables the user to send data, information, or control signals to a com puter. The Central Processing Unit (CPU) of a computer receives the input and processes it to produce the output.

Some of the popular input devices are:

1. Keyboard
2. Mouse
3. Scanner
4. Joystick
5. Light Pen
6. Digitizer
7. Microphone
8. Magnetic Ink Character Recognition (MICR)
9. Optical Character Reader (OCR)
10. Digital Camera
11. Paddle
12. Steering Wheel
13. Gesture recognition devices
14. Light Gun
15. Touch Pad
16. Remote
17. Touch screen
18. VR
19. Webcam
20. Biometric Devices

1) Keyboard

The keyboard is a basic input device that is used to enter data into a computer or any other electronic device by pressing keys. It has different sets of keys for letters, numbers, characters, and functions. Keyboards are connected to a computer through USB or a Bluetooth device for wireless communication.

Types of keyboards: There can be different types of keyboards based on the region and language used. Some of the common types of keyboards are as follows:

i) QWERTY Keyboard:

It is the most commonly used keyboard with computers in modern times. It is named after the first six letters of the top row of buttons and is even popular in countries that do not use Latin-based alphabet. It is so popular that some people think that it is the only type of keyboard to use with computers as an input device.

ii) AZERTY Keyboard:

It is considered the standard French keyboard. It is developed in France as an alternative layout to the QWERTY layout and is mainly used in France and other European countries. Some countries have manufactured their own versions of AZERTY.

Its name is derived from the first six letters that appear on the top left row of the keyboard. The Q and W keys in AZERTY keyboard are interchanged with A and Z keys in QWERTY keyboard. Furthermore, in AZERTY keyboard M key is located to the left of the L key.

AZERTY keyboard differs from QWERTY keyboard not only in the placement of letters but also in many other ways, e.g., it gives emphasis on accents, which is required for writing European languages like French.

iii) DVORAK Keyboard:

This type of keyboard layout was developed to increase the typing speed by reducing the finger movement while typing. The most frequently used letters are kept in a home row to improve typing.

2) Mouse The mouse is a hand-held input device which is used to move cursor or pointer across the screen. It is designed to be used on a flat surface and generally has left and right button and a scroll wheel between them. Laptop computers come with a touchpad that works as a mouse. It lets you control the movement of cursor or pointer by moving your finger over the touchpad. Some mouse comes with integrated features such as extra buttons to perform different buttons.

The mouse was invented by Douglas C. Engelbart in 1963. Early mouse had a roller ball integrated as a movement sensor underneath the device. Modern mouse devices come with optical technology that controls cursor movements by a visible or invisible light beam. A mouse is connected to a computer through different ports depending on the type of computer and type of a mouse.

Common types of the mouse:

i) Trackball Mouse:

It is a stationary input device that has ball mechanism to move the pointer or cursor on the screen. The ball is half inserted in the device and can be easily rolled with finger, thumb or the palm to move the pointer on the screen. The device has sensor to detect the rotation of ball. It remains stationary; you don't need to move it on the operating surface. So, it is an ideal device if you have limited desk space as you don't need to move it like a mouse.

ii) Mechanical Mouse:

It has a system of a ball and several rollers to track its movement. It is a corded type of mouse. A mechanical mouse can be used for high performance. The drawback is that they tend to get dust into the mechanics and thus require regular cleaning.

iii) Optical Mouse:

An optical mouse uses optical electronics to track its movement. It is more reliable than a mechanical mouse and also requires less maintenance. However, its performance is affected by the surface on which it is operated. Plain non-glossy mouse mat should be used for best results. The rough surface may cause problems for the optical recognition system, and the glossy surface may reflect the light wrongly and thus may cause tracking issues.

iv) Cordless or Wireless Mouse:

As the name suggests, this type of mouse lacks cable and uses wireless technology such as IrDA (infrared) or radio (Bluetooth or Wi-Fi) to control the movement of the cursor. It is used to improve the experience of using a mouse. It uses batteries for its power supply.

3) Scanner

The scanner uses the pictures and pages of text as input. It scans the picture or a document. The scanned picture or document then converted into a digital format or file and is displayed on the screen as an output. It uses optical character recognition techniques to convert images into digital ones. Some of the common types of scanners are as follows:

Types of Scanner:

i) Flatbed Scanner:

It has a glass pane and a moving optical CIS or CCD array. The light illuminates the pane, and then the image is placed on the glass pane. The light moves across the glass pane and scans the document and thus produces its digital copy. You will need a transparency adapter while scanning transparent slides.

ii) Handheld Scanner:

It is a small manual scanning device which is held by hand and is rolled over a flat image that is to be scanned. The drawback in using this device is that the hand should be steady while scanning; otherwise, it may distort the image. One of the commonly used handheld scanners is the barcode scanner which you would have seen in shopping stores.

iii) Sheetfed Scanner:

In this scanner, the document is inserted into the slot provided in the scanner. The main components of this scanner include the sheet-feeder, scanning module, and calibration sheet. The light does not move in this scanner.

Instead, the document moves through the scanner. It is suitable for scanning single page documents, not for thick objects like books, magazines, etc.

iv) Drum Scanner:

Drum scanner has a photomultiplier tube (PMT) to scan images. It does not have a charge-coupled device like a flatbed scanner. The photomultiplier tube is extremely sensitive to light. The image is placed on a glass tube, and the light moves across the image, which produces a reflection of the image which is captured by the PMT and processed. These scanners have high resolution and are suitable for detailed scans.

v) Photo Scanner:

It is designed to scan photographs. It has high resolution and color depth, which are required for scanning photographs. Some photo scanners come with in-built software for cleaning and restoring old photographs.

4) Joystick

A joystick is also a pointing input device like a mouse. It is made up of a stick with a spherical base. The base is fitted in a socket that allows free movement of the stick. The movement of stick controls the cursor or pointer on the screen.

The frist joystick was invented by C. B. Mirick at the U.S. Naval Research Laboratory. A joystick can be of different types such as displacement joysticks, finger-operated joysticks, hand operated, isometric joystick, and more. In joystick, the cursor keeps moving in the direction of the joystick unless it is upright, whereas, in mouse, the cursor moves only when the mouse moves.

5) Light Pen

A light pen is a computer input device that looks like a pen. The tip of the light pen contains a light-sensitive detector that enables the user to point to or select objects on the display screen. Its light sensitive tip detects the object location and sends the corresponding signals to the CPU. It is not compatible with LCD screens, so it is not in use today. It also helps you draw on the screen if needed. The first light pen was invented around 1955 as a part of the Whirlwind project at the Massachusetts Institute of Technology (MIT).

6) Digitizer

Digitizer is a computer input device that has a flat surface and usually comes with a stylus. It enables the user to draw images and graphics using the stylus as we draw on paper with a pencil. The images or graphics drawn on the digitizer appear on the computer monitor or display screen. The software converts the touch inputs into lines and can also convert handwritten text to typewritten words.

It can be used to capture handwritten signatures and data or images from taped papers. Furthermore, it is also used to receive information in the form of drawings and send output to a CAD (Computer-aided design) application and software like AutoCAD. Thus, it allows you to convert hand-drawn images into a format suitable for computer processing.

7) Microphone

The microphone is a computer input device that is used to input the sound. It receives the sound vibrations and converts them into audio signals or sends to a recording medium. The audio signals are converted into digital data and stored in the computer. The microphone also enables the user to telecommunicate with others. It is also used to add sound to presentations and with webcams for video conferencing. A microphone can capture audio waves in different ways; accordingly the three most common types are described below:

8) Magnetic Ink Character Recognition (MICR)

MICR computer input device is designed to read the text printed with magnetic ink. MICR is a character recognition technology that makes use of special magnetized ink which is sensitive to magnetic fields. It is widely used in banks to process the cheques and other organizations where security is a major concern. It can process three hundred cheques in a minute with hundred-percent accuracy. The details on the bottom of the cheque (MICR No.) are written with magnetic ink. A laser printer with MICR toner can be used to print the magnetic ink. The device reads the details and sends to a computer for processing. A document printed in magnetic ink is required to pass through a machine which magnetizes the ink, and the magnetic information is then translated into characters.

9) Optical Character Reader (OCR)

OCR computer input device is designed to convert the scanned images of handwritten, typed or printed text into digital text. It is widely used in offices and libraries to convert documents and books into electronic files.

It processes and copies the physical form of a document using a scanner. After copying the documents, the OCR software converts the documents into a two-color (black and white), version called bitmap. Then it is analyzed for light and dark areas, where the dark areas are selected as characters, and the light area is identified as background. It is widely used to convert hard copy legal or historic documents into PDFs. The converted documents can be edited if required like we edit documents created in ms word.

10) Paddle:

It is a simple input device that is widely used in games. It is a wheel that is held by hand and looks like a volume knob on a stereo that is used to increase or decrease the volume. Paddle moves or controls cursor or any other objects in the game in a back-and-forth motion. It is widely used as an alternative to the joystick. Besides this, the term paddle also refers to many handheld devices designed to control a function in an electronic device, computer, etc.

11) Touchpad:

It is usually found in laptops as a substitute for the mouse. It allows you to move or control the cursor on the screen using your finger. Just like a mouse, it also has two buttons for right and left click. Using the touchpad, you can perform all the tasks that you do with a mouse, such as selecting an object on the screen, copy, paste, delete, open a file or folder, and more.

12) Touch screen:

It is the display screen of a device such as a smartphone, tablet, etc., that allows users to interact or provide inputs to the device by using their finger. Today, most of the electronic devices come with touchscreen as an alternative to a mouse for navigating a graphical user interface. For example, by touching, you can unlock your phone, open emails, open files, play videos, etc. Besides this, it is used in lots of devices such as Camera, Car GPS, Fitness machine, etc.

The concept of the touch screen was first introduced and published by E.A. Johnson in 1965. The first touch screen was developed at the beginning of the 1970s by CERN engineers Frank Beck and Bent Stumpe.

13) Webcam:

Any camera which is connected to a computer is called a webcam. The in-built camera provided on a computer can also be considered a webcam. It is an input device as it can take pictures, and can be used to record videos if required. The pictures and videos are stored in the computer memory and can be displayed on the screen if required. Although it works almost the same as the digital camera, it is different from a digital camera, as it is designed to take compact digital photos that can be uploaded easily on the webpages and shared with others through the internet.

Biometric Devices:

Biometrics refers to a process in which a person is identified through his or her biological features such as fingerprints, eye cornea, face structure, etc. It is done by using biometric devices, which can be of different types based on their scanning features and abilities, such as:

i) Face Scanner:

It is designed to identify a person by scanning his or her face. It takes the face measurements of a person. For example, the distance between eyes, nose, and mouth, etc., accordingly, it confirms the identity of a person. Besides this, it is smart enough to differentiate between a person's picture and the real person.

ii) Hand Scanner:

The hand of a person can also be used to verify his or her identity as every person has a unique pattern of veins in the palm, just like fingerprints. This device takes advantage of this feature; it identifies a person by scanning the palm of his hand. It uses infrared light to scan veins' patterns and blood flowing in them. Palm is even more unique than fingerprints.

iii) Fingerprint Scanner:

It scans the fingerprints to identify people or for biometric authentication. This device is developed, keeping in mind the fact that no two persons in the world can have the same fingerprints. It is widely used in companies as a fingerprint attendance system to mark the attendance of employees. This type of scanners captures the pattern of valleys and ridges found on a finger and store it in the memory or database. When you press your finger on the given space, it verifies the identity by using its pattern-matching software.

iv) Retina or Iris Scanner:

It scans the retina or iris of a person's eye to confirm the identity. This device is more secure than others as it is next to impossible to copy the retina or iris. It works by mapping the retina's blood vessel patterns of the eye. The blood vessels of retina absorb light more easily as well as can be identified with appropriate lighting.

In this scan, a beam of low-energy infrared light falls on the retina through the scanner's eyepiece. Then, the software captures the network of blood vessels in the retina and uses it to verify a person's identity.

v) Voice Scanner:

It records the voice of a person and digitizes it to create a distinctive voice print or template. The voiceprints are stored in the database, and are used to verify the voice of a person to confirm his or her identity. The person is required to speak in the normal or same voice that was used to create a voice template. It is not much reliable as it can be misused using a tape recording.

Output Devices

The output device displays the result of the processing of raw data that is entered in the computer through an input device. There are a number of output devices that display output in different ways such as text, images, hard copies, and audio or video.

1) Monitor

The monitor is the display unit or screen of the computer. It is the main output device that displays the processed data or information as text, images, audio or video.

The types of monitors are given below.

i) CRT Monitor

CRT monitors are based on the cathode ray tubes. They are like vacuum tubes which produce images in the form of video signals. Cathode rays tube produces a beam of electrons through electron guns that strike on the inner phosphorescent surface of the screen to produce images on the screen. The monitor contains millions of phosphorus dots of red, green and blue color. These dots start to glow when struck by electron beams and this phenomenon is called cathodoluminescence.

The main components of a CRT monitor include the electron gun assembly, deflection plate assembly, fluorescent screen, glass envelope, and base.The front (outer surface) of the screen onto which images are produced is called the face plate. It is made up of fiber optics.

There are three electron beams that strike the screen: red, green, and blue. So, the colors which you see on the screen are the blends of red, blue and green lights.The magnetic field guides the beams of electrons. Although LCDs have replaced the CRT monitors, the CRT monitors are still used by graphics professionals because of their color quality.

ii) LCD Monitor

The LCD monitor is a flat panel screen that is compact and light-weight as compared to CRT monitors. It is based on liquid crystal display technology which is used in the screens of laptops, tablets, smart phones, etc. An LCD screen comprises two layers of polarized glass with a liquid crystal solution between them. When the light passes through the first layer, an electric current aligns the liquids crystals. The aligned liquid crystals allow a varying level of light to pass through the second layer to create images on the screen.

The LCD screen has a matrix of pixels that display the image on the screen.Old LCDs had passive-matrix screens in which individual pixels are controlled by sending a charge. A few electrical charges could be sent each second that made screens appear blurry when the images moved quickly on the screen.

Modern LCDs use active-matrix technology and contain thin film transistors (TFTs) with capacitors. This technology allows pixels to retain their charge. So, they don?t make screen blurry when images move fast on the screen as well as are more efficient than passive-matrix displays.

iii) LED monitor

The LED monitor is an improved version of an LCD monitor. It also has a flat panel display and uses liquid crystal display technology like the LCD monitors. The difference between them lies in the source of light to backlight the display. The LED monitor has many LED panels, and each panel has several LEDsto backlight the display, whereas the LCD monitors use cold cathode fluorescent light to backlight the display.Modern electronic devices such as mobile phones, LED TVs, laptop and computer screens, etc., use a LED display as it not only produces more brilliance and greater light intensity but also consumes less power.

iv) Plasma Monitor

The plasma monitor is also a flat panel display that is based on plasma display technology. It has small tiny cells between two glass panels. These cells contain mixtures of noble gases and a small amount of mercury. When voltage is applied, the gas in the cells turns into a plasma and emits ultraviolet light that creates images on the screen, i.e., the screen is illuminated by a tiny bit of plasma, a charged gas. Plasma displays are brighter than liquid crystal displays (LCD) and also offer a wide viewing angle than an LCD.

Plasma monitors provide high resolutions of up to 1920 X 1080, excellent contrast ratios, wide viewing angle, a high refresh rate and more. Thus, they offer a unique viewing experience while watching action movies, sports games, and more.

2) Printer

A printer produces hard copies of the processed data. It enables the user, to print images, text or any other information onto the paper.

Based on the printing mechanism, the printers are of two types: Impact Printers and Non-impact Printers.

Impact Printer

The impact printer uses a hammer or print head to print the character or images onto the paper. The hammer or print head strikes or presses an ink ribbon against the paper to print characters and images.

Impact printers are further divided into two types.

A. Character Printers

B. Line printers

A) Character Printers

Character printer prints a single character at a time or with a single stroke of the print head or hammer. It does not print one line at a time. Dot Matrix printer and Daisy Wheel printer are character printers. Today, these printers are not in much use due to their low speed and because only the text can be printed. The character printers are of two types, which are as follows:

i) Dot Matrix Printer

Dot Matrix Printer is an impact printer. The characters and images printed by it are the patterns of dots. These patterns are produced by striking the ink soaked ribbon against the paper with a print head. The print head contains pins that produce a pattern of dots on the paper to form the individual characters. The print head of a 24 pin dot matrix contains more pins than a 9 pin dot matrix printer, so it produces more dots which results in better printing of characters. To produce color output, the black ribbon can be changed with color stripes. The speed of Dot Matrix printers is around 200-500 characters per second.

ii) Daisy Wheel Printer

Daisy Wheel Printer was invented by David S. Lee at Diablo Data Systems.It consists of a wheel or disk that has spokes or extensions and looks like a daisy, so it is named Daisy Wheel printer. At the end of extensions, molded metal characters are mounted. To print a character the printer rotates the wheel, and when the desired character is on the print location the hammer hits disk and the extension hits the ink ribbon against the paper to create the impression. It cannot be used to print graphics and is often noisy and slow, i.e., the speed is very low around 25-50 characters per second. Due to these drawbacks,these printers have become obsolete.

B) Line Printers:

Line printer, which is also as a bar printer, prints one line at a time. It is a high-speed impact printer as it can print 500 to 3000 lines per minute. Drum printer and chain printer are examples of line printers.

i) Drum Printer:

Drum printer is a line printer that is made of a rotating drum to print characters. The drum has circular bands of characters on its surface. It has a separate hammer for each band of characters. When you print, the drum rotates, and when the desired character comes under the hammer, the hammer strikes the ink ribbon against the paper to print characters. The drum rotates at a very high speed and characters are printed by activating the appropriate hammers. Although all the characters are not printed at a time, they are printed at a very high speed. Furthermore, it can print only a predefined style as it has a specific set of characters. These printers are known to be very noisy due to the use of hammering techniques.

ii) Chain Printer:

Chain printer is a line printer that uses a rotating chain to print characters. The characters are embossed on the surface of the chain. The chain rotates horizontally around a set of hammers, for each print location one hammer is provided, i.e., the total number of hammers is equal to the total number of print positions.

The chain rotates at a very high speed and when the desired character comes at the print location, the corresponding hammer strikes the page against the ribbon and character on the chain.They can type 500 to 3000 lines per minute. They are also noisy due to the hammering action.

Non-Impact Printer:

Non-impact printers don't print characters or images by striking a print head or hammer on the ink ribbon placed against the paper. They print characters and images without direct physical contact between the paper and the printing machinery. These printers can print a complete page at a time, so they are also known as page printers. The common types of non-impact printers are Laser printer and Inkjet printer:

i) Laser Printer:

A laser printer is a non-impact printer that uses a laser beam to print the characters. The laser beam hits the drum, which is a photoreceptor and draws the image on the drum by altering electrical charges on the drum. The drum then rolls in toner, and the charged image on the drum picks the toner. The toner is then printed on the paper using heat and pressure. Once the document is printed, the drum loses the electric charge,and the remaining toner is collected. The laser printers use powdered toner for printing instead of liquid ink and produce quality print objects with a resolution of 600 dots per inch (dpi) or more.

ii) Inkjet Printer:

The inkjet printer is a non-impact printer that prints images and characters by spraying fine,ionized drops of ink. The print head has tiny nozzles to spray the ink. The printer head moves back and forth and sprays ionized drops of ink on the paper, which is fed through the printer. These drops pass through an electric field that guides the ink onto the paper to print correct images and characters.

An inkjet printer has cartridges that contain ink. Modern inkjet printers are color printers that have four cartridges containing different colors: Cyan, Magenta, Yellow, and Black. It is capable of printing high-quality images with different colors. It can produce print objects with a resolution of at least 300 dots per inch (dpi).

3) Projector

A projector is an output device that enables the user to project the output onto a large surface such as a big screen or wall. It can be connected to a computer and similar devices to project their output onto a screen. It uses light and lenses to produce magnified texts, images, and videos. So, it is an ideal output device to give presentations or to teach a large number of people.

Modern projects (digital projectors) come with multiple input sources such as HDMI ports for newer equipment and VGA ports that support older devices. Some projectors are designed to support Wi-Fi and Bluetooth as well. They can be fixed onto the ceiling, placed on a stand, and more and are frequently used for classroom teaching, giving presentations, home cinemas, etc.

A digital projector can be of two types:

Liquid Crystal Display (LCD) digital projector: This type of digital projectors are very popular as they are lightweight and provide crisp output. An LCD projector uses transmissive technology to produce output. It allows the light source, which is a standard lamp, to pass through the three colored liquid crystal light panels. Some colors pass through the panels and some are blocked by the panels and thus images are on the screen.

Digital Light Processing (DLP) digital projector: It has a set of tiny mirrors, a separate mirror for each pixel of the image and thus provide high-quality images. These projectors are mostly used in theatres as they fulfill the requirement of high-quality video output.

Central Processing Unit (CPU)

A Central Processing Unit is also called a processor, central processor, or microprocessor. It carries out all the important functions of a computer. It receives instructions from both the hardware and active software and produces output accordingly. It stores all important programs like operating systems and application software. CPU also helps Input and output devices to communicate with each other. Owing to these features of CPU, it is often referred to as the brain of the computer.

CPU is installed or inserted into a CPU socket located on the motherboard. Furthermore, it is provided with a heat sink to absorb and dissipate heat to keep the CPU cool and functioning smoothly.

Generally, a CPU has three components:

- ALU (Arithmetic Logic Unit)
- Control Unit
- Memory or Storage Unit

Control Unit: It is the circuitry in the control unit, which makes use of electrical signals to instruct the computer system for executing already stored instructions. It takes instructions from memory and then decodes and executes these instructions. So, it controls and coordinates the functioning of all parts of the computer. The Control Unit's main task is to maintain and regulate the flow of information across the processor. It does not take part in processing and storing data.

ALU: It is the arithmetic logic unit, which performs arithmetic and logical functions. Arithmetic functions include addition, subtraction, multiplication division, and comparisons. Logical functions mainly include selecting, comparing, and merging the data. A CPU may contain more than one ALU. Furthermore, ALUs can be used for maintaining timers that help run the computer.

Memory or Storage Unit/ Registers: It is called Random access memory (RAM). It temporarily stores data, programs, and intermediate and final results of processing. So, it acts as a temporary storage area that holds the data temporarily, which is used to run the computer.

What is CPU Clock Speed?

The clock speed of a CPU or a processor refers to the number of instructions it can process in a second. It is measured in gigahertz. For example, a CPU with a clock speed of 4.0 GHz means it can process 4 billion instructions in a second.

Types of CPU:

CPUs are mostly manufactured by Intel and AMD, each of which manufactures its own types of CPUs. In modern times, there are lots of CPU types in the market. Some of the basic types of CPUs are described below:

Single Core CPU: Single Core is the oldest type of computer CPU, which was used in the 1970s. It has only one core to process different operations. It can start only one operation at a time; the CPU switches back and forth between different sets of data streams when more than one program runs. So, it is not suitable for multitasking as the performance will be reduced if more than one application runs. The performance of these CPUs is mainly dependent on the clock speed. It is still used in various devices, such as smartphones.

Dual Core CPU: As the name suggests, Dual Core CPU contains two cores in a single Integrated Circuit (IC). Although each core has its own controller and cache, they are linked together to work as a single unit and thus can perform faster than the single-core processors and can handle multitasking more efficiently than Single Core processors.

Quad Core CPU: This type of CPU comes with two dual-core processors in one integrated circuit (IC) or chip. So, a quad-core processor is a chip that contains four independent units called cores. These cores read and execute instructions of CPU. The cores can run multiple instructions simultaneously, thereby increases the overall speed for programs that are compatible with parallel processing.

Quad Core CPU uses a technology that allows four independent processing units (cores) to run in parallel on a single chip. Thus by integrating multiple cores in a single CPU, higher performance can be generated without boosting the clock speed. However, the performance increases only when the computer's software supports multiprocessing. The software which supports multiprocessing divides the processing load between multiple processors instead of using one processor at a time.

History of CPU:

Some of the important events in the development of CPU since its invention till date are as follows:

- In 1823, Baron Jons Jackob Berzelius discovered silicon that is the main component of CPU till date.
- In 1903, Nikola Tesla got gates or switches patented, which are electrical logic circuits.
- In December 1947, John Bardeen, William Shockley, and Walter Brattain invented the first transistor at the Bell Laboratories and got it patented in 1948.
- In 1958, the first working integrated circuit was developed by Robert Noyce and Jack Kilby.
- In 1960, IBM established the first mass-production facility for transistors in New York.
- In 1968, Robert Noyce and Gordon Moore founded Intel Corporation.
- AMD (Advanced Micro Devices) was founded in May 1969.
- In 1971, Intel introduced the first microprocessor, the Intel 4004, with the help of Ted Hoff.
- In 1972, Intel introduced the 8008 processor; in 1976, Intel 8086 was introduced, and in June 1979, Intel 8088 was released.
- In 1979, a 16/32-bit processor, the Motorola 68000, was released. Later, it was used as a processor for the Apple Macintosh and Amiga computers.
- In 1987, Sun introduced the SPARC processor.
- In March 1991, AMD introduced the AM386 microprocessor family.
- In March 1993, Intel released the Pentium processor. In 1995, Cyrix introduced the Cx5x86 processor to give competition to Intel Pentium processors.
- In January 1999, Intel introduced the Celeron 366 MHz and 400 MHz processors.
- In April 2005, AMD introduced its first dual-core processor.
- In 2006, Intel introduced the Core 2 Duo processor.
- In 2007, Intel introduced different types of Core 2 Quad processors.
- In April 2008, Intel introduced the first series of Intel Atom processors, the Z5xx series. They were single-core processors with a 200 MHz GPU.

- In September 2009, Intel released the first Core i5 desktop processor with four cores.
- In January 2010, Intel released many processors such as Core 2 Quad processor Q9500, first Core i3 and i5 mobile processors, first Core i3 and i5 desktop processors. In the same year in July, it released the first Core i7 desktop processor with six cores.
- In June 2017, Intel introduced the first Core i9 desktop processor.
- In April 2018, Intel released the first Core i9 mobile processor.

What is Computer Hardware?

Hardware, which is abbreviated as HW, refers to all physical components of a computer system, including the devices connected to it. You cannot create a computer or use software without using hardware. The screen on which you are reading this information is also a hardware.

What is a hardware upgrade?

A hardware upgrade refers to a new hardware, or a replacement for the old one, or additional hardware developed to improve the performance of the existing hardware. A common example of a hardware upgrade is a RAM upgrade that increases the computer's total memory, and video card upgrade, where the old video card is removed and replaced with the new one.

Computer Hardware Parts

Some of the commonly used hardware in your computer are described below:

1. Motherboard
2. Monitor
3. Keyboard
4. Mouse

1) Motherboard:

The motherboard is generally a thin circuit board that holds together almost all parts of a computer except input and output devices. All crucial hardware like CPU, memory, hard drive, and ports for input and output devices are located on the motherboard. It is the biggest circuit board in a computer chassis.

It allocates power to all hardware located on it and enables them to communicate with each other. It is meant to hold the computer's microprocessor chip and let other components connect to it. Each component that runs the computer or improves its performance is a part of the motherboard or connected to it through a slot or port.

There can be different types of motherboards based on the type and size of the computers. So, a specific motherboard can work only with specific types of processors and memory.

Components of a Motherboard:

CPU Slot: It is provided to install the CPU. It is a link between a microprocessor and a motherboard. It facilitates the use of CPU and prevents the damage when it is installed or removed. Furthermore, it is provided with a lock to prevent CPU movement and a heat sink to dissipate the extra heat.

RAM Slot: It is a memory slot or socket provided in the motherboard to insert or install the RAM (Random Access Memory). There can be two or more memory slots in a computer.

Expansion Slot: It is also called the bus slot or expansion port. It is a connection or port on the motherboard, which provides an installation point to connect a hardware expansion card, for example, you can purchase a video expansion card and install it into the expansion slot and then can install a new video card in the computer. Some of the common expansion slots in a computer are AGP, AMR, CNR, PCI, etc.

Capacitor: It is made of two conductive plates, and a thin insulator sandwiched between them. These parts are wrapped in a plastic container.

Inductor (Coil): It is an electromagnetic coil made of a conducting wire wrapped around an iron core. It acts as an inductor or electromagnet to store magnetic energy.

Northbridge: It is an integrated circuit that allows communications between the CPU interface, AGP, and memory. Furthermore, it also allows the southbridge chip to communicate with the RAM, CPU, and graphics controller.

USB Port: It allows you to connect hardware devices like mouse, keyboard to your computer.

PCI Slot: It stands for Peripheral Component Interconnect slot. It allows you to connect the PCI devices like modems, network hardware, sound, and video cards.

AGP Slot: It stands for Accelerated Graphics Port. It provides the slot to connect graphics cards.

Heat Sink: It absorbs and disperses the heat generated in the computer processor.

Power Connector: It is designed to supply power to the motherboard.

CMOS battery: It stands for complementary metal-oxide-semiconductor. It is a memory that stores the BIOS settings such as time, date, and hardware settings.

2) Monitor:

A monitor is the display unit of a computer on which the processed data, such as text, images, etc., is displayed. It comprises a screen circuity and the case which encloses this circuity. The monitor is also known as a visual display unit (VDU).

Types of Monitors:

1. **CRT Monitor:** It has cathode ray tubes which produce images in the form of video signals. Its main components are electron gun assembly, deflection plate assembly, glass envelope, fluorescent screen, and base.
2. **LCD Monitor:** It is a flat panel screen. It uses liquid crystal display technology to produce images on the screen. Advanced LEDs have thin-film transistors with

capacitors and use active-matrix technology, which allows pixels to retain their charge.

3. **LED Monitor:** It is an advanced version of an LCD monitor. Unlike an LCD monitor, which uses cold cathode fluorescent light to backlight the display, it has LED panels, each of which has lots of LEDs to display the backlight.
4. **Plasma Monitor:** It uses plasma display technology that allows it to produce high resolutions of up to 1920 X 1080, wide viewing angle, a high refresh rate, outstanding contrast ration, and more.

3) Keyboard:

It is the most important input device of a computer. It is designed to allow you input text, characters, and other commands into a computer, desktop, tablet, etc. It comes with different sets of keys to enter numbers, characters, and perform various other functions like copy, paste, delete, enter, etc.

A keyboards is an input device through which users can input text, numbers, and special characters. It is an input device with a typical QWERTY keyset. It is an external hardware device that is connected to the computer. It serves as the user's most fundamental interface with a system. It has numerous buttons that can be used to generate letters, numbers, and symbols as well as unique keys like the Windows and Alt keys that can also accomplish other tasks.

Types of Keyboards:

1. QWERTY Keyboards
2. AZERTY Keyboards
3. DVORAK Keyboards

4) Mouse:

It is a small handheld device designed to control or move the pointer (computer screen's cursor) in a GUI (graphical user interface). It allows you to point to or select objects on a computer's display screen. It is generally placed on a flat surface as we need to move it smoothly to control the pointer. Types of Mouse: Trackball mouse, Mechanical Mouse, Optical Mouse, Wireless Mouse, etc.

A mouse can be wireless or wired. It is a portable pointing device that is used to interact with objects on computer screens with the help of moving the cursor around the screen. On the display screen, the cursor moves in the same direction as the users' mouse movements. The term "mouse" refers to a compact, wired, elliptical-shaped gadget that somewhat resembles a mouse.

Main functions of a mouse:

- **Move the cursor:** It is the main function of the mouse; to move the cursor on the screen.
- **Open or execute a program:** It allows you to open a folder or document and execute a program. You are required to take the cursor on the folder and double click it to open it.
- **Select:** It allows you to select text, file, or any other object.
- **Hovering:** Hovering is an act of moving the mouse cursor over a clickable object. During hovering over an object, it displays information about the object without pressing any button of the mouse.
- **Scroll:** It allows you to scroll up or down while viewing a long webpage or document.

Parts of a mouse:

- **Two buttons:** A mouse is provided with two buttons for right click and left click.
- **Scroll Wheel:** A wheel located between the right and left buttons, which is used to scroll up and down and Zoom in and Zoom out in some applications like AutoCAD.
- **Battery:** A battery is required in a wireless mouse.
- **Motion Detection Assembly:** A mouse can have a trackball or an optical sensor to provide signals to the computer about the motion and location of the mouse.

What are external hardware components?

The items that are frequently attached to the computer from outside in order to control input or output functions are known as external hardware components, sometimes known as peripheral components. These hardware components either serve as input devices for the software or output devices for the output of the software's operations (output).

The following are examples of common input hardware components:

Microphone: A microphone is an input device that converts sound waves into electrical impulses in order to allow computer-based audio communications. It was developed by Emile Berliner in **1877**. It is used to enter audio into computers or transform sound waves into electric waves. It captures audio with the help of converting sound waves into an electrical signal that could be a digital or analog signal. This process can be implemented by a computer as well as other digital audio devices.

USB flash drive: A USB flash drive is a type of storage device for data that connects to a computer via a USB port and uses flash memory. It is an external, removable storage device that has a built-in Universal Serial Bus (USB) interface. Many USB flash drives can be removed and written to. They have a compact, reliable, and small physical design. They often operate more quickly the more storage space they have. Because there are no moving parts, USB flash drives are extremely mechanically durable.

Memory card: A memory card is a kind of portable external storage device; video, photo, and other data files can be stored on it. A form of storage medium, which is additionally known as a flash memory. Also, it provides a volatile and non-volatile medium. It is frequently found in gadgets, including phones, laptops, digital cameras, camcorders, gaming consoles, MP3 players, printers, and more.

Joysticks, styluses, and scanners are examples of additional input hardware components.

The following are a few examples of output hardware components:

Printer: A printer is a hardware output device used to produce hard copies of documents or print them. It converts computer-generated electronic data into printed form. Text files, pictures, or a combination of the two can all be considered documents. It receives input commands from users so that computers or other devices may print the sheets. You must create a soft copy of your report and print it using a printer, for example, if your institution needs you to submit a project report.

Speaker: One of the most popular output devices is a speaker that connects to a computer to generate a sound output. While some speakers can only be connected to computers, others can be used with any type of sound system.

Headphones, earphones, earbuds: These are also output devices much like speakers, which offer audio that can only be heard by one listener.

Hardware vs. software

Hardware describes the physical parts of the computer or its delivery mechanisms that hold and execute the software's written instructions. The intangible component of the system software enables the user to communicate with the hardware and give commands to perform specific tasks. Computer software includes:

- OS and associated tools;
- Applications that regulate particular computer operations
- Programs that generally operate on data provided by the user

Virtual keyboards are not physical keyboards; therefore, they are also considered software on mobile devices and laptop computers.

The software must be developed to function properly with the hardware because they both are necessary for a computer to create usable output. Also, they depend on each other.

If any system has malware or malicious software, such as worms, spyware, viruses, and Trojan horses, they can have a significant impact on software and the operating system of a system. Malware, however, has no effect on hardware.

On the other hand, malware can impact the system in additional ways. For example, it can use up a lot of memory of the system or even reproduce itself to take up the entire hard drive. This can stop reliable programs from working and causes the computer to run slowly. Furthermore, users may not be able to access the files stored on the computer's hardware due to malware.

What is hardware virtualization?

The abstraction of physical computing resources from the software that utilizes those resources is known as hardware virtualization. Put on another way; hardware virtualization is the process of creating virtual representations of hardware by using software rather than physical, tangible hardware components for various computing functions.

A particular hardware platform by host software is used to execute hardware virtualization, and it is sometimes referred to as platform or server virtualization. It needs a hypervisor, a virtual machine manager that turns internal hardware into virtual forms. As a result, among OSes and applications, the hardware resources of one physical machine can be shared easily and used more efficiently.

In cloud computing, infrastructure as a service (IaaS), a delivery model that offers hardware resources over high-speed internet, is frequently associated with hardware virtualization.

All of the hardware elements that are typically found in an on-premises data center, including servers, storage, and networking hardware, as well as the software that enables virtualization, are hosted by a cloud service provider (CSP), such as Amazon Web Services or Microsoft Azure.

IaaS and CSPs differ from hardware as a service (HaaS) providers in that they don't host software but only host hardware. A typical IaaS provider also offers a variety of services to go along with infrastructure parts, like the following:

- billing
- clustering
- log access
- monitoring
- security
- load balancing

Other storage resilience services are also provided by some CSPs, including disaster recovery, automated backup, and replication.

What is hardware as a service?

While buying computer hardware and occasionally replacing or upgrading it is common for individuals or businesses. People and businesses can also rent physical and virtual hardware from a service provider. The maintenance of the hardware, including all of its numerous physical parts and the software that runs on them, becomes the responsibility of the service provider. It is also called the HaaS model.

The most significant advantage of HaaS is it decreases the price of purchasing and maintaining hardware, allowing businesses to switch from a capital expenditure budget to a typically cheaper operational expense budget. Additionally, the majority of HaaS options are based on a pay-as-you-go model, which makes it simpler for businesses in order to manage expenditures while still having access to the hardware they require for their operational and business continuity.

HaaS involves installing physical parts that belong to a managed service provider (MSP) at a client's location. The responsibilities of both parties are defined by an SLA (service-level agreement).

For using the MSP's hardware, the customer may either pay a monthly cost or have it included in the MSP's fee schedule for setting up, maintaining, and monitoring the hardware. In either case, the MSP is in charge of fixing or replacing the hardware if it breaks down or becomes outdated.

Decommissioning hardware may involve physically destroying hard drives, deleting confidential data, and verifying that used equipment has been recycled legally on the basis of the SLA's requirements.

Computer hardware problems and diagnostics methods

In modern times, troubleshooting computer hardware issues has become more convenient, faster, and easier as well. You can quickly determine which equipment is having problems if you have the correct IT inventory management tool.

The effectiveness of management procedures is greatly improved by automated IT inventory management software. You can deliver the best services by correlating, analyzing, and tracking changes with the help of these tools for asset management. They enable you to produce detailed records and define maintenance timeframes, which make it simpler to track the performance of each asset and reduce the need for manual updates.

The software has the ability to monitor hardware warranty, and expiration dates in addition to tracking and identifying hardware faults. These functions assist you in service level agreements, organizing upcoming purchases, and procurement plans in accordance with corporate requirements. The asset automatically updates the inventory as necessary if it finds configuration changes and performance issues. Software for managing hardware inventories can perform the following things, for example:

- Immediately gather IT inventory data and auto-discover assets.
- Send immediate warnings regarding CPU and motherboard hardware problems or when your operating system, firmware, and software upgrades are available.
- Keep track of any server operating system upgrades.
- Track and manage the maintenance requirements and life cycles of the hardware inventory
- Also, with powerful IT inventory management software, you can identify and monitor configuration changes.

FAQs on Computer Hardware

1. What is the Hardware of a Computer?

All of a computer's tangible and physical parts are referred to as its hardware, which is abbreviated as HW. This implies that hardware can refer to any component that can be viewed or touched. Hardware is required to build a computer and run the software. This information is displayed on a screen, which is hardware.

2. What are the Five Types of Hardware?

Below is a list of the five different types of hardware.

- Keyboard
- Motherboard
- Mouse

- CPU (Central Processing Unit)
- Monitor

3. How is computer hardware dependent on software?

Consider the hardware of a computer as a human body that contains numerous visible and touchable body parts. But the body cannot move or carry out its role if there is no soul inside of it. And it would be seen as having expired or will be considered dead.

Similar to this, a structure is provided by the computer hardware; it includes input and output devices, such as a keyboard, mouse, monitor, etc. But software is also very necessary for the system because it will not work if it has not had the necessary software to carry out its intended tasks. Consequently, they are both dependent on one another.

4. Why do we need to study computer hardware?

Hardware topics for the computer are covered as early as classes 5 and 7. Students gradually start studying more in-depth information about the subject as they go to higher standards. The primary objective of learning this material is to teach students the fundamentals of building, maintaining, and repairing computer systems. They ought to be able to recognize and differentiate between hardware and software.

5. Is RAM a part of a computer hardware system?

You will learn about RAM or random-access memory when you study the inside parts of computer hardware, which is a memory socket fitted into the computer's motherboard. These slots for memory are external; in order to store additional data, we can even place two memory slots. As a result, RAM is now a physical component of computer hardware.

6. How is RAM different from ROM?

In a computer system, memory slots for both RAM and ROM are present. Random access memory, or RAM, is a type of volatile memory that is used to store data momentarily. On the other hand, ROM is non-volatile memory storage and a form of permanent, which stands for real only memory.

Read the complete article on the Javatpoint website for a thorough explanation of RAM and ROM from the subject matter specialists.

7. Is the topic of computer hardware difficult to remember?

If you study with more attention and clarity, no subject is challenging to learn. When you start reading about computer hardware, you can easily learn the subject of computer hardware because it is quite straightforward and simple to learn. The subject matter specialists at Javatpoint break down complex concepts into manageable chunks, which makes it straightforward for students to understand even when they are going to learn it for the first time. The main objective we have in common at Javatpoint is that studying should not be a burden and learning should be enjoyable. Therefore, learn any subject with us that you find challenging and see how simple it becomes after learning.

Software

Software, which is abbreviated as SW or S/W, is a set of programs that enables the hardware to perform a specific task. All the programs that run the computer are software. The software can be of three types: system software, application software, and programming software.

1) System Software

The system software is the main software that runs the computer. When you turn on the computer, it activates the hardware and controls and coordinates their functioning. The application programs are also controlled by system software. An operating system is an example of system software.

i) Operating System:

An operating system is the system software that works as an interface to enable the user to communicate with the computer. It manages and coordinates the functioning of hardware and software of the computer. The commonly used operating systems are Microsoft Windows, Linux, and Apple Mac OS X.

Some other examples of system software include:

BIOS: It stands for basic input output system. It is a type of system software, which is stored in Read Only Memory (ROM) located on the motherboard. However, in advanced computer systems, it is stored in flash memory. BIOS is the first software that gets activated when you turn on your computer system. It loads the drivers of the hard disk into memory as well as assists the operating system to load itself into the memory.

Boot Program: Boot refers to starting up a computer. When you switch on the computer, the commands in the ROM are executed automatically to load the boot program into memory and execute its instructions. The BIOS program has a basic set of commands that enables the computer to perform the basic input/output instructions to start the computer.

An assembler: It plays the role of a converter as it receives basic computer instructions and converts them into a pattern of bits. The proccssor uses these bits to perform basic operations.

A device driver: This system software controls hardware devices connected to a computer. It enables the computer to use the hardware by providing an appropriate interface. The kernel of a Computer's CPU communicates with different hardware through this software.

Operating systems generally come with most of the device drivers. If the operating system does not have a device driver for hardware, you have to install the device driver before using that hardware device.

2) Application Software:

Application software is a set of programs designed to perform a specific task. It does not control the working of a computer as it is designed for end-users. A computer can run without application software. Application software can be easily installed or uninstalled as required. It can be a single program or a collection of small programs.

Microsoft Office Suite, Adobe Photoshop, and any other software like payroll software or income tax software are application software. As we know, they are designed to perform specific tasks. Accordingly, they can be of different types such as:

Word Processing Software: This software allows users to create, edit, format, and manipulate the text and more. It offers lots of options for writing documents, creating images, and more. For example, MS Word, WordPad, Notepad, etc.

Spreadsheet Software: It is designed to perform calculations, store data, create charts, etc. It has rows and columns, and the data is entered in the cell, which is an intersection of a row and column, e.g., Microsoft Excel.

Multimedia Software: These software are developed to perform editing of video, audio, and text. It allows you to combine texts, videos, audio, and images. Thus, you can improve a text document by adding photos, animations, graphics, and charts through multimedia software. For example, VLC player, Window Media Player, etc.

Enterprise Software: These software are developed for business operational functions. It is used in large organizations where the quantum of business is too large. It can be used for accounting, billing, order processing and more. For example, CRM (Customer Relationship Management), BI (Business Intelligence), ERP (Enterprise Resource Planning), SCM (Supply Chain Management), customer support system, and more.

3) Programming Software:

It is a set or collection of tools that help developers in writing other software or programs. It assists them in creating, debugging, and maintaining software or programs or applications. We can say that these are facilitator software that helps translate programming language such as Java, C++, Python, etc., into machine language code. So, it is not used by end-users. For example, compilers, linkers, debuggers, interpreters, text editors, etc. This software is also called a programming tool or software development tool.

Some examples of programming software include:

- **Eclipse:** It is a java language editor.
- **Coda:** It is a programming language editor for Mac.
- **Notepad++:** It is an open-source editor for windows.
- **Sublime text:** It is a cross-platform code editor for Linux, Mac, and Windows.

Operating System Tutorial

Operating System Tutorial provides the basic and advanced concepts of operating system . Our Operating system tutorial is designed for beginners, professionals and GATE aspirants. We have designed this tutorial after the completion of a deep research about every concept.

The content is described in detailed manner and has the ability to answer most of your queries. The tutorial also contains the numerical examples based on previous year GATE questions which will help you to address the problems in a practical manner.

Operating System can be defined as an interface between user and the hardware. It provides an environment to the user so that, the user can perform its task in convenient and efficient way.

The Operating System Tutorial is divided into various parts based on its functions such as Process Management, Process Synchronization, Deadlocks and File Management.

Operating System Definition and Function

In the Computer System (comprises of Hardware and software), Hardware can only understand machine code (in the form of 0 and 1) which doesn't make any sense to a naive user. We need a system which can act as an intermediary and manage all the processes and resources present in the system.

An **Operating System** can be defined as an **interface between user and hardware**. It is responsible for the execution of all the processes, Resource Allocation, CPU management, File Management and many other tasks. The purpose of an operating system is to provide an environment in which a user can execute programs in convenient and efficient manner.

Structure of a Computer System

A Computer System consists of:

- Users (people who are using the computer)

- Application Programs (Compilers, Databases, Games, Video player, Browsers, etc.)
- System Programs (Shells, Editors, Compilers, etc.)
- Operating System (A special program which acts as an interface between user and hardware)
- Hardware (CPU, Disks, Memory, etc)

What does an Operating system do?

1. Process Management
2. Process Synchronization
3. Memory Management
4. CPU Scheduling
5. File Management
6. Security

Types of Operating Systems (OS)

An operating system is a well-organized collection of programs that manages the computer hardware. It is a type of system software that is responsible for the smooth functioning of the computer system.

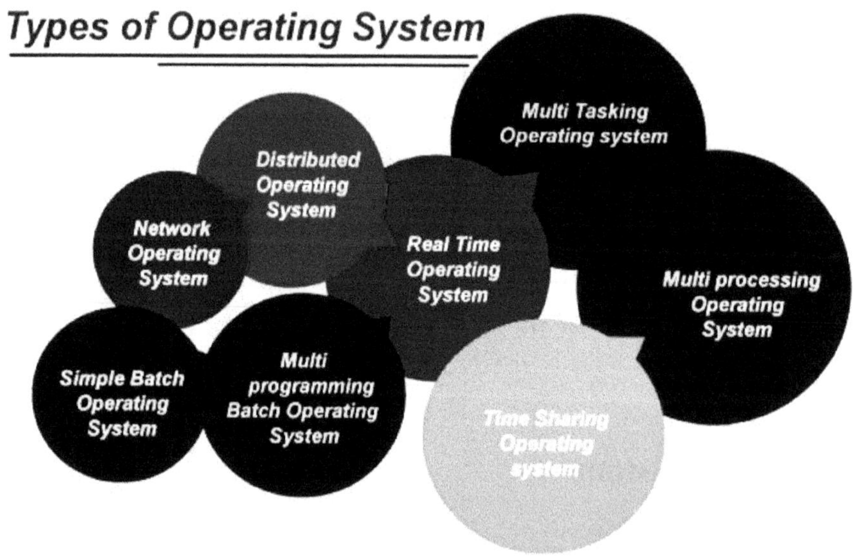

Batch Operating System

In the 1970s, Batch processing was very popular. In this technique, similar types of jobs were batched together and executed in time. People were used to having a single computer which was called a mainframe.

In Batch operating system, access is given to more than one person; they submit their respective jobs to the system for the execution.

The system put all of the jobs in a queue on the basis of first come first serve and then executes the jobs one by one. The users collect their respective output when all the jobs get executed.

The purpose of this operating system was mainly to transfer control from one job to another as soon as the job was completed. It contained a small set of programs called the resident monitor that always resided in one part of the main memory. The remaining part is used for servicing jobs.

2. Not Interactive Batch Processing is not suitable for jobs that are dependent on the user's input. If a job requires the input of two numbers from the console, then it will never get it in the batch processing scenario since the user is not present at the time of execution.

Multiprogramming Operating System

Multiprogramming is an extension to batch processing where the CPU is always kept busy. Each process needs two types of system time: CPU time and IO time.

In a multiprogramming environment, when a process does its I/O, The CPU can start the execution of other processes. Therefore, multiprogramming improves the efficiency of the system.

Advantages of Multiprogramming OS

- Throughout the system, it increased as the CPU always had one program to execute.
- Response time can also be reduced.

Disadvantages of Multiprogramming OS

Multiprogramming systems provide an environment in which various systems resources are used efficiently, but they do not provide any user interaction with the computer system.

Multiprocessing Operating System

In Multiprocessing, Parallel computing is achieved. There are more than one processors present in the system which can execute more than one process at the same time. This will increase the throughput of the system.

In Multiprocessing, Parallel computing is achieved. More than one processor present in the system can execute more than one process simultaneously, which will increase the throughput of the system.

Advantages of Multiprocessing operating system:

Increased reliability: Due to the multiprocessing system, processing tasks can be distributed among several processors. This increases reliability as if one processor fails, the task can be given to another processor for completion.

Increased throughout: As several processors increase, more work can be done in less.

Disadvantages of Multiprocessing operating System

Multiprocessing operating system is more complex and sophisticated as it takes care of multiple CPUs simultaneously.

Multitasking Operating System

The multitasking operating system is a logical extension of a multiprogramming system that enables **multiple** programs simultaneously. It allows a user to perform more than one computer task at the same time.

Advantages of Multitasking operating system

- This operating system is more suited to supporting multiple users simultaneously.

- The multitasking operating systems have well-defined memory management.

Disadvantages of Multitasking operating system

The multiple processors are busier at the same time to complete any task in a multi-tasking environment, so the CPU generates more heat.

Network Operating System

Advantages of Network Operating System

- In this type of operating system, network traffic reduces due to the division between clients and the server.
- This type of system is less expensive to set up and maintain.

Disadvantages of Network Operating System

- In this type of operating system, the failure of any node in a system affects the whole system.
- Security and performance are important issues. So trained network administrators are required for network administration.

Real Time Operating System

In Real-Time Systems, each job carries a certain deadline within which the job is supposed to be completed, otherwise, the huge loss will be there, or even if the result is produced, it will be completely useless.

The Application of a Real-Time system exists in the case of military applications, if you want to drop a missile, then the missile is supposed to be dropped with a certain precision.

Advantages of Real-time operating system:

- Easy to layout, develop and execute real-time applications under the real-time operating system.
- In a Real-time operating system, the maximum utilization of devices and systems.

Disadvantages of Real-time operating system:

- Real-time operating systems are very costly to develop.

- Real-time operating systems are very complex and can consume critical CPU cycles.

Time-Sharing Operating System

In the Time Sharing operating system, computer resources are allocated in a time-dependent fashion to several programs simultaneously. Thus it helps to provide a large number of user's direct access to the main computer. It is a logical extension of multiprogramming. In time-sharing, the CPU is switched among multiple programs given by different users on a scheduled basis.

A time-sharing operating system allows many users to be served simultaneously, so sophisticated CPU scheduling schemes and Input/output management are required.

Advantages of Time Sharing Operating System

- The time-sharing operating system provides effective utilization and sharing of resources.
- This system reduces CPU idle and response time.

Disadvantages of Time Sharing Operating System

- Data transmission rates are very high in comparison to other methods.
- Security and integrity of user programs loaded in memory and data need to be maintained as many users access the system at the same time.

Distributed Operating System

The Distributed Operating system is not installed on a single machine, it is divided into parts, and these parts are loaded on different machines. A part of the distributed Operating system is installed on each machine to make their communication possible. Distributed Operating systems are much more complex, large, and sophisticated than Network operating systems because they also have to take care of varying networking protocols.

Advantages of Distributed Operating System

- The distributed operating system provides sharing of resources.
- This type of system is fault-tolerant.

Disadvantages of Distributed Operating System

Protocol overhead can dominate computation cost.

Process Management in OS

A Program does nothing unless its instructions are executed by a CPU. A program in execution is called a process. In order to accomplish its task, process needs the computer resources.

There may exist more than one process in the system which may require the same resource at the same time. Therefore, the operating system has to manage all the processes and the resources in a convenient and efficient way.

Some resources may need to be executed by one process at one time to maintain the consistency otherwise the system can become inconsistent and deadlock may occur.

The operating system is responsible for the following activities in connection with Process Management.

FUTURE OF COMPUTERS

Modern computers are found everywhere: homes, offices, businesses, hospitals, and schools, to name a few. Contemporary society has become so dependent on computers that many people become frustrated and unable to function when computers are "down." Because of this dependence, computers are regarded as essential tools for everything from navigation to entertainment.

Today's computers are smaller, faster, and cheaper than their predecessors. Some computers are the size of a deck of cards. Hand-held Personal Data Assistants and notebook computers or "ultra-lights" make users portable and give them the opportunity to work in a variety of places. These systems provide a wide range of connectivity and access to information on local, wide, and wireless networks. This gives users more convenience and more control over their time.

Future computers promise to be even faster than today's computers and smaller than a deck of cards. Perhaps they will become the size of coins and offer "smart" or artificial intelligence features like expert intelligence, neural network pattern recognition features, or natural language capabilities. These capabilities will allow users to more conveniently interact with systems and efficiently process large amounts of information from a variety of sources: fax, e-mail, Internet, and telephone. Already evident are some evolving cutting-edge applications for computer technology: wearable computers, DNA computers, virtual reality devices, quantum computers, and optical computers.

Wearable Computers

Is a wearable computer in your future? With hardware shrinking and becoming more powerful and more able to execute instructions and perform computations in shorter timeframes, it is very possible that there will be widespread use of wearable systems in the future. A wearable is defined as a handless system with a data processor supported by a user's body rather than an external surface. The unit may have several components (camera, touch panel, screen, wrist-mounted keyboard, head-worn display, and so forth) that work together to bring technology to situational and environmental problems.

Assembly and repair environments are ideally suited for wearable technology because they deploy users with technical expertise to problem areas. Wearable computers allow users to keep their hands free at all times while providing access to technical specifications and detailed instructions for problem-solving and troubleshooting.

In the future, wearables may even be built into the fabric of clothing. Garments can be made using conductive and nonconductive textiles like organza and yarn, gripper snaps, and embroidered elements. Ordinary fabric can be connected to electronic components to add functionality and usability.

DNA-Based Computers

Can small molecules such as DNA be used as the basis for new computing devices? A biologist and mathematician named Leonard Adelman first linked genetics and computer technology in the mid-1990s. Adelman coded a problem using the four nucleotides that combine to form DNA and discovered that the DNA solution was accurate. A DNA-based computer would be radically different from a conventional computer. Instead of storing data on silicon chips, converting data to binary notation (0s and 1s), and performing computations on the binary digits, DNA computing would rely on data found in patterns of molecules in a synthetic DNA strand.

Each strand represents one possible answer to the problem. A set of strands is manufactured so that all conceivable answers are included. To winnow out a solution, the DNA computer subjects all the strands simultaneously to a series of chemical reactions that imitate mathematical computations.

The advantage of DNA computing is that it works in parallel, processing all possible answers simultaneously. An electronic computer can analyze only one potential answer at a time. The future holds great possibilities as DNA-based computers could be used to perform parallel processing applications, DNA fingerprinting , and the decoding of strategic information such as banking, military, and communications data.

Virtual Reality Devices

Virtual reality (VR) immerses its user in a simulated world of possibilities and actions. In the virtual world, the user has the ability (through head-mounted displays, gloves, and body suits) to respond to tactile stimulation. Users manipulate objects, examine architectural renderings, and interact in an environment before it becomes a physical reality. This is often very cost-effective, and it supports decision-making tasks. VR is often used in modeling situations, but its future holds promise in other areas: education, government, medicine, and personal uses.

In education, students and teachers may have the ability to interact inside virtual classrooms to explore ideas, construct knowledge structures, and conduct experiments without risk, fear of failure, or alienation. Government offices may use VR technology to improve services, provide better delivery of health care (model symptoms, progression, and prevention), and monitor environmental changes in air quality, wetlands, ozone layers, and other ecological areas (animal populations and forestry).

Medical areas could use VR to train interns and practicing physicians on new procedures and equipment; observe internal tissue production in three dimensions (3-D); collect and better analyze medical images; simulate surgical and invasive procedures; and empower therapists to use exposure therapy along with realistic models. VR technology could also be used to augment instructional games, 3-D movies, and real-time conferencing and communication efforts.

Quantum Computers

The first application of quantum theory and computers occurred in 1981 at Argonne National Laboratory. Quantum computers, like conventional computing systems, were proposed before supportive hardware existed. In 1985, a quantum parallel computer was proposed. Today, physicists and computer scientists still hope that the imprecision of subatomic particles can be used to solve problems that thus far remain unsolved.

The quantum computer would overcome some of the problems that have plagued conventional computers: namely, sequentially following rules and representing data as a series of switches corresponding to 0 or 1. By using subatomic particles, quantum computers will have the ability to represent a number of different states simultaneously. These particles will be manipulated by the rules of probability rather than absolute states or logic gates. Manipulating these small subatomic particles will allow researchers to solve larger, more complex problems, such as determining drug properties, performing complex computations, precisely predicting weather conditions, and helping chip designers create circuits that are presently impossibly complex.

Optical Computers

As microprocessor chip designers reach physical limitations that prevent them from making chips faster, they are searching for other materials to conduct data through the electrical circuits of computer systems. If designers could harness photons to transmit data, faster microprocessor chips could become a reality.

This new frontier—optical computing—could allow computers to perform parallel processing tasks more efficiently and increase the speed and complexity of computers by allowing them to process billions of bits simultaneously. Optical computers might use fiber-optic cable, optical chips, or wireless optical networks to process and transmit data.

Fiber-optic cable is currently used in many establishments. It uses a laser to transmit billions of data bits through cables made of thin strands of glass coated in layers of plastic. Signals can be carried over a distance of 40 to 60 miles. A more recent development—optical chips—could cut the cost of optical communication by using Dense Wave Division Multiplexing technology to carry more information over a fiber. This would give users increased bandwidth for connecting to the Internet. Optical networks could be used to improve free-space optics, video delivery, and voice communications.

First Generation Computers

Computers have come a long way since their inception in the 1940s. Back then, between the period 1940 to 1956, First Generation Computers were staggeringly big and ran on steam engines! They relied heavily on **magnetic drums** for storage and vacuum tubes as switches/amplifiers – which produced considerable amounts of heat requiring coolers to regulate them. To program these beasts, machine language was used – although rudimentary by today's standards it was groundbreaking at the time.

Recommended for you: The Most Notorious Computer Viruses in Our History.

Second Generation Computers

The Second Generation of computers was a quantum leap in computer technology between 1956 to 1963. Upgrading from the bulky, power-hungry vacuum tubes of First Generation machines to smaller, more efficient transistors allowed for improved performance and reduced energy consumption.

The memory base moved away from simply magnetic storage and incorporated core memories, leading to less heat production while simultaneously improving speed capabilities. With this new advancement in size came an increased capacity for automation that had never been seen before – paving the way for even more significant advancements yet still unknown!

Third Generation Computers

With the introduction of computers between 1964 and 1971, a technological revolution was born! Taking leaps compared to previous generations in terms of speed, storage capacity, and size – semiconductor chips or **integrated circuits** played an integral role. For the first time ever, users could interact with their computing devices through keyboards as well as mouses. This marked a true game-changer for humanity's relationship with technology – speeding up progress faster than we'd believed possible until then!

Fourth Generation Computers

The Fourth Generation of Computers, spanning from 1971 to 2010 brought about the exciting introduction of Personal Computers or PCs. Altair 8800 marked a groundbreaking moment in technology- these powerful computers required assembly before use and featured Intel 4004 chips with millions of transistors – heralding an unprecedented era for computing capabilities! Taking computing to the next level, computers became revolutionized during the 70s and 80s. Pre-assembled machines such as the Commodore Pet in 1978 and Apple II of 1977 made their way into households around the world. This marked a new era for personal home use with IBM'sPC setting precedent soon after. Moreover, by connecting systems together over networks – the internet was born! Computers achieved remarkable developments by introducing greater memory capacity, and data storage options alongside considerable miniaturization resulting in handy handheld devices we look down at today! Propelling further influence on modern-day users is a Fourth Generation of Computer technology that brought about a **Graphical User Interface** (GUI), producing an easier method of visual interactivity compared to predecessors it stands beside.

Fifth Generation Computers

Computer technology is undergoing a tremendous transformation with unprecedented advances. We can only imagine the possibilities that quantum, AI, and nanotechnology offer for computing power! What we are witnessing today in computer development will surely be just a taste of what's to come – an exciting time ahead as computers enter into new-age technologies.

The Internet of Things (IoT)

Imagine a future where you can command your appliances from anywhere else in the world – no need to be at home! This radical notion is made possible by the **Internet of Things** (IoT) technology, making devices smarter and more connected than ever before.

With IoT, computers are able to communicate autonomously with each other like never seen before – it's truly revolutionary! Imagine living in a world where cars start on their own, ovens know when to turn off and bicycles greet you with an automated "hello" when they sense your watch.

The future of computers has much more potential than we ever imagined – enter the Internet of Things! This technology will make homes smarter, cities better managed, schools safer and hospitals run like well-oiled machines.

With this mind-boggling connectivity between devices powered by computer software, it's easy to see just how efficient our day-to-day lives can become due to the power of 'smart' communication.

Bio-Computers

Make way for the newest medical marvels- bio-computers! Imagine taking a computer not just as small as an aspirin, but actually swallowing it like one. Or, getting a chip implanted in your hand to constantly monitor any unexpected changes in your DNA cells? Believe it or not, this is no longer science fiction – these amazing new technologies are closer than ever and will revolutionize healthcare by providing cutting-edge solutions for biotechnology fields.

Imagine a computer that is much, much smaller than it currently exists and doesn't just offer tremendous processing power but can even learn by itself! This will be possible with **Bio-computers** of the future which have biological and organic elements running processes to store data.

With such technology available in the near future, there are endless possibilities for how we could use this new form of computing – from detecting abnormalities or badly structured DNA to providing large benefits both economically and socially.

BASIC KNOWLEDGE OF THE INTERNET

Introduction

The **Internet** is an increasingly important part of everyday life for people around the world. But if you've never used the Internet before, all of this new information might feel a bit confusing at first.

Throughout this tutorial, we'll try to answer some basic questions you may have about the Internet and how it's used. When you're done, you'll have a good understanding of **how the Internet works**, how to **connect to the Internet**, and **how to browse the Web**.

What is the Internet?

The Internet is a global network of billions of computers and other electronic devices. With the Internet, it's possible to access almost any information, communicate with anyone else in the world, and do much more.

You can do all of this by connecting a computer to the Internet, which is also called going online. When someone says a computer is online, it's just another way of saying it's connected to the Internet.

What is thc Web?

The **World Wide Web**—usually called the **Web** for short—is a collection of different **websites** you can access through the Internet. A **website** is made up of related text, images, and other resources. Websites can resemble other forms of media—like newspaper articles or television programs—or they can be interactive in a way that's unique to computers.

The purpose of a website can be almost anything: a news platform, an advertisement, an online library, a forum for sharing images, or an educational site like us!

Once you are connected to the Internet, you can access and view websites using a type of application called a **web browser**. Just keep in mind that the web browser itself is not the Internet; it only displays websites that are stored on the Internet.

How does the Internet work?

At this point you may be wondering, **how does the Internet work?** The exact answer is pretty complicated and would take a while to explain. Instead, let's look at some of the most important things you should know.

It's important to realize that the Internet is a global network of **physical cables**, which can include copper telephone wires, TV cables, and fiber optic cables. Even wireless connections like Wi-Fi and 3G/4G rely on these physical cables to access the Internet.

When you visit a website, your computer sends a request over these wires to a **server**. A server is where websites are stored, and it works a lot like your computer's hard drive. Once the request arrives, the server retrieves the website and sends the correct data back to your computer. What's amazing is that this all happens in just a few seconds!

Other things you can do on the Internet

One of the best features of the Internet is the ability to communicate almost instantly with anyone in the world. **Email** is one of the oldest and most universal ways to communicate and share information on the Internet, and billions of people use it. **Social media** allows people to connect in a variety of ways and build communities online.

There are many other things you can do on the Internet. There are thousands of ways to keep up with news or **shop for anything** online. You can pay your bills, **manage your bank accounts**, meet new people, **watch TV**, or learn new skills. You can learn or do almost anything online.

Introduction

There's almost no limit to what you can do online. The Internet makes it possible to quickly find information, communicate with people around the world, manage your finances, shop from home, listen to music, watch videos, and much, much more. Let's take a look at some of the ways the Internet is most commonly used today.

Finding information online

With billions of websites online today, there is **a lot** of information on the Internet. **Search engines** make this information easier to find. All you have to do is type one or more **keywords**, and the search engine will look for **relevant websites**.

For example, let's say you're looking for a new pair of shoes. You could use a search engine to learn about different types of shoes, get directions to a nearby shoe store, or even find out where to buy them online!

Email

Short for electronic mail, **email** is a way to **send and receive messages** across the Internet. Almost everyone who uses the Internet has their own email account, usually called an **email address**. This is because you'll need an email address to do just about anything online, from online banking to creating a Facebook account.

Social networking

Social networking websites are another way to **connect and share** with your family and friends online. Rather than sharing with just a few people over email, social networks make it easier to **connect** and **share** with many people at the same time. **Facebook** is the world's largest social networking site, with **more than 1 billion users** worldwide.

Chat and instant messaging

Chat and **instant messaging (IM)** are short messages sent and read **in real time**, allowing you to converse more quickly and easily than email. These are generally used when both (or all) people are online, so your message can be read immediately. By comparison, **emails** won't be seen until recipients check their inboxes.

Examples of instant messaging applications include **Yahoo Messenger** and **Google Hangouts**. Some sites, like **Gmail** and **Facebook**, even allow you to chat within your web browser.

Online media

There are many sites that allow you to **watch videos** and **listen to music**. For example, you can watch millions of videos on **YouTube** or listen to Internet radio on **Pandora**. Other services, like **Netflix** and **Hulu**, allow you to watch movies and TV shows. And if have a **set-top streaming box**, you can even watch them directly on your television instead of a computer screen.

Everyday tasks

You can also use the Internet to complete many **everyday tasks** and **errands**. For example, you can manage your bank account, pay your bills, and shop for just about anything. The main advantage here is **convenience**. Rather than going from place to place, you can do all of these tasks at home!

And a whole lot more!

Remember, these are just a few of the things you'll be able to do online. Keep working through this tutorial to learn more about connecting to the Internet and using the Web!

How do I connect to the Internet?

Once you've set up your computer, you may want to purchase **home Internet access** so you can send and receive email, browse the Web, stream videos, and more. You may even want to set up a **home wireless network**, commonly known as **Wi-Fi**, so you can connect multiple devices to the Internet at the same time.

Types of Internet service

The type of Internet service you choose will largely depend on which **Internet service providers** (ISPs) serve your area, along with the types of service they offer. Here are some common types of Internet service.

Dial-up: This is generally the slowest type of Internet connection, and you should probably avoid it unless it is the only service available in your area. Dial-up Internet uses your **phone line**, so unless you have multiple phone lines you will not be able to use your landline and the Internet at the same time.

DSL: DSL service uses a **broadband connection**, which makes it much faster than dial-up. DSL connects to the Internet **via a phone line** but does not require you to have a landline at home. And unlike dial-up, you'll be able to use the Internet and your phone line at the same time.

Cable: Cable service connects to the Internet **via cable TV**, although you do not necessarily need to have cable TV in order to get it. It uses a broadband connection and can be faster than both dial-up and DSL service; however, it is only available where cable TV is available.

Satellite: A satellite connection uses broadband but does not require cable or phone lines; it connects to the Internet **through satellites orbiting the Earth**. As a result, it can be used almost anywhere in the world, but the connection may be affected by weather patterns. Satellite connections are also usually slower than DSL or cable.

3G and 4G: 3G and 4G service is most commonly used with mobile phones, and it connects **wirelessly** through your ISP's network. However, these types of connections aren't always as fast as DSL or cable. They will also **limit the amount of data** you can use each month, which isn't the case with most broadband plans.

Choosing an Internet service provider

Now that you know about the different types of Internet service, you can do some research to find out what ISPs are available in your area. If you're having trouble getting started, we recommend talking to friends, family members, and neighbors about the ISPs they use. This will usually give you a good idea of the types of Internet service available in your area.

Most ISPs offer several tiers of service with different Internet speeds, usually measured in **Mbps** (short for **megabits per second**). If you mainly want to use the Internet for **email** and **social networking**, a slower connection (around 2 to 5 Mbps) might be all you need. However, if you want to **download music** or **stream videos**, you'll want a faster connection (at least 5 Mbps or higher).

You'll also want to **consider the cost** of the service, including installation charges and monthly fees. Generally speaking, the faster the connection, the more expensive it will be per month.

Hardware needed

Modem

Once you have your computer, you really don't need much additional hardware to connect to the Internet. The primary piece of hardware you need is a **modem**.

The type of Internet access you choose will determine the type of modem you need. **Dial-up** access uses a **telephone modem**, **DSL** service uses a **DSL modem**, **cable** access uses a **cable modem**, and **satellite** service uses a **satellite adapter**. Your ISP may give you a modem—often for a fee—when you sign a contract, which helps ensure that you have the **right type** of modem. However, if you would prefer to shop for a **better** or **less expensive** modem, you can choose to buy one separately.

Router

A **router** is a hardware device that allows you to connect **several computers** and **other devices** to a single Internet connection, which is known as a **home network**. Many routers are **wireless**, which allows you to create a **home wireless network**, commonly known as a **Wi-Fi network**.

You **don't necessarily need to buy a router** to connect to the Internet. It's possible to connect your computer directly to your modem using an Ethernet cable. Also, many modems include a **built-in router**, so you have the option of creating a Wi-Fi network without buying extra hardware.

Setting up your Internet connection

Once you've chosen an ISP, most providers will **send a technician to your house** to turn on the connection. If not, you should be able to use the instructions provided by your ISP—or included with the modem—to set up your Internet connection.

After you have everything set up, you can open your **web browser** and begin using the Internet. If you have any problems with your Internet connection, you can call your ISP's **technical support** number.

Home networking

If you have multiple computers at home and want to use all of them to access the Internet, you may want to create a **home network**, also known as a **Wi-Fi network**. In a home network, all of your devices connect to your **router**, which is connected to the **modem**. This means everyone in your family can use the Internet **at the same time**.

Your ISP technician may be able to set up a home Wi-Fi network when installing your Internet service. If not, you can review our lesson on **How to Set Up a Wi-Fi Network** to learn more.

If you want to connect a computer that does not have built-in Wi-Fi connectivity, you can purchase a **Wi-Fi adapter** that plugs into your computer's USB port.

What is the cloud?

You may have heard people using terms like **the cloud**, **cloud computing**, or **cloud storage**. But what exactly is the cloud?

Simply put, the cloud is **the Internet**—more specifically, it's all of the things you can **access remotely** over the Internet. When something is **in the cloud**, it means it's stored on **Internet servers** instead of your computer's hard drive.

Why use the cloud?

Some of the main reasons to use the cloud are **convenience** and **reliability**. For example, if you've ever used a **web-based email service**, such as **Gmail** or **Yahoo! Mail**, you've already used the cloud. All of the emails in a web-based service are stored on servers rather than on your computer's hard drive. This means you can access your email from any computer with an Internet connection. It also means you'll be able to recover your emails if something happens to your computer.

File storage: You can store all types of information in the cloud, including files and email. This means you can access these things from **any computer** or **mobile device** with an Internet connection, not just your home computer. **Dropbox** and **Google Drive** are some of the most popular cloud-based storage services.

What is a web app?

Previously, we talked about how **desktop applications** allow you to perform tasks on your computer. But there are also **web applications**—or **web apps**—that run **in the cloud** and do not need to be installed on your computer. Many of the most popular sites on the Internet are actually web apps. You may have even used a web app without realizing it! Let's take a look at some popular web apps.

Facebook: Facebook lets you create an online **profile** and interact with your **friends**. Profiles and conversations can be updated at any time, so Facebook uses web app technologies to **keep the information up to date**.

Pixlr: Pixlr is an **image editing application** that runs in your web browser. Much like **Adobe Photoshop**, it includes many advanced features, like color correction and sharpening tools.

Google Docs: Google Docs is an **office suite** that runs in your browser. Much like **Microsoft Office**, you can use it to create **documents**, **spreadsheets**, **presentations**, and more. And because the files are stored **in the cloud**, it's easy to **share** them with others.

Using a web browser

A **web browser** is a type of software that allows you to find and view websites on the Internet. Even if you didn't know it, you're using a web browser right now to read this page! There are many different web browsers, but some of the most common ones include **Google Chrome**, **Safari**, and **Mozilla Firefox**.

No matter which web browser you use, you'll want to learn the basics of browsing the Web. In this lesson, we'll talk about **navigating** to different websites, **using tabbed browsing**, creating **bookmarks**, and more.

URLs and the address bar

Each website has a unique address, called a **URL** (short for **Uniform Resource Locator**). It's like a street address that tells your browser where to go on the Internet. When you type a URL into the browser's **address bar** and press **Enter** on your keyboard, the browser will load the page associated with that URL.

Links

Whenever you see a word or phrase on a website that's **blue** or **underlined in blue**, it's probably a **hyperlink**, or **link** for short. You might already know how links work, even if you've never thought about them much before. For example, try clicking the link below.

Tabbed browsing

Many browsers allow you to open links in a new **tab**. You can open as many links as you want, and they'll stay in the **same browser window** instead of cluttering your screen with multiple windows.

To open a link in a new tab, **right-click** the link and select **Open link in new tab** (the exact wording may vary from browser to browser).

Bookmarks and history

If you find a website you want to view later, it can be hard to memorize the exact web address. **Bookmarks**, also known as **favorites**, are a great way to save and organize specific websites so you can revisit them again and again. Simply locate and select the **Star** icon to bookmark the current website.

Your browser will also keep a history of every site you visit. This is another good way to find a site you visited previously. To view your history, open your browser settings—usually by clicking the icon in the upper-right corner—and select **History**.

Downloading files

Links don't always go to another website. In some cases, they point to a **file** that can be **downloaded**, or saved, to your computer.

If you click a link to a file, it may download automatically, but sometimes it just **opens within your browser** instead of downloading. To prevent it from opening in the browser, you can **right-click** the link and select **Save link as** (different browsers may use slightly different wording, like **Save target as**).

Uploading

If a site allows uploads, it will have an upload utility to help perform the file transfer. Each site handles this process differently, but we'll give some common examples. Usually, the site will have help pages to walk you through the upload process.

Many sites have an upload button that opens a dialog box. For example, Facebook has a camera icon that begins the upload process.

NETWORKING SOFTWARE & HARDWARE

What Is Network Software?

Network software is an umbrella term used to describe a wide range of software that streamlines the operations, design, monitoring, and implementation of computer networks.

Network software is a fundamental element for any networking system. It helps administrators and security personnel reduce network complexities, and manage, monitor, and better control network traffic. Network software plays a crucial role in managing a network infrastructure and simplifying IT operations by facilitating communication, security, content, and data sharing.

Network software offers useful benefits to organizations. It has become an important tool in facilitating round-the-clock communication and allowing an uninterrupted exchange of information. One of the most significant advantages of network software is its direct correlation with productivity. The centralized nature of network software increases the productivity of the complete system. This helps reduce end-user technical support problems.

For example, if an end user accidentally damages their computer, the chances of losing data are reduced substantially as all its data is already shared on the network. Another key benefit of network software is its ability to enable programmatic management of network resources. This eliminates the need for manual processes, thereby providing a dynamic and efficient network configuration to work with.

Functions of network software

User management allows administrators to add or remove users from the network. This is particularly useful when hiring or relieving

File management lets administrators decide the location of data storage and control user access to that data.

Access enables users to enjoy uninterrupted access to network resources.

Network security systems assist administrators in looking after security and preventing data breaches.

Although, it is important to note that traditional networks were hardware-based and comprised elements such as routers and switches with embedded software. The decoupling of software from hardware, called software-defined networking (SDN), works exceptionally well to simplify the management of infrastructure, making it more adaptable to the constantly evolving course of the tech world. The introduction of SDN has been a turning point and has completely changed the way networking is done.

See More: What Is Network Access Control? Definition, Key Components and Best Practices

Key Components of Network Software

Network software is an advanced, robust, and secure alternative to traditional networking, making the network easier to administer in terms of management, modifications, configuration, supply resources, and troubleshooting. The use of network software makes it possible to administer from one centralized user interface while completely eliminating the need to acquire additional hardware. It offers administrators the option to customize with greater flexibility to change and define the network speed, expand network capacity, and look after security.

To understand how it works, let's look at the components that frame network software.

1. Application layer

The first component is the application layer or the application plane, which refers to the applications and services running on the network. It is a program that conveys network information, the status of the network, and the network requirements for particular resource availability and application. This is done through the control layer via application programming interfaces (APIs). The application layer also consists of the application logic and one or more API drivers.

2. Control layer

The control layer lies at the center of the architecture and is one of the most important components of the three layers. You could call it the brain of the whole system. Also called the controller or the control plane, this layer also includes the network control software and the network operating system within it. It is the entity in charge of receiving requirements from the applications and translating the same to the network components. The control of the infrastructure layer or the data plane devices is also done via the controller. In simple terms, the control layer is the intermediary that facilitates communication between the top and bottom layers through APIs interfaces.

3. Infrastructure layer

The infrastructure layer, also called the data plane, consists of the actual network devices (both physical and virtual) that reside in this layer. They are primarily responsible for moving or forwarding the data packets after receiving due instructions from the control layer. In simple terms, the data plane in the network architecture components physically handles user traffic based on the commands received by the controller.

The application program interface (API) ties all three components together. Communication between these three layers is facilitated through northbound and southbound application program interfaces. The northbound API ties communication between the application and the control layers, whereas the southbound API enables communication between the infrastructure and the control layers.

1. Northbound API

Applications communicate to the controller to present the status of the network infrastructure and request resources based on availability. This communication between the application and the control layer happens via northbound APIs that help instruct what resources the application requires and routes them to the destination in question.

Northbound APIs are majorly RESTful APIs. The control layer decides how the applications are allotted the resources available in the network. Through its automated intelligence, the control layer also finds an ideal route for the application as per its latency and security.

2. Southbound API

The control layer communicates with the infrastructure layer (routers and switches) via southbound APIs. The network infrastructure is informed about the route the application data must move on based on the configurations made by the controller. The controller can control and change how the routers and switches move the data.

A major difference between traditional network software architecture and SDN architecture is that the former's control and infrastructure layers are integrated. This only allows limited changes to the overall system as the network devices become an obstruction in the logical network traffic flow. On the other hand, SDN separates the control layer from the infrastructure layer and centrally integrates the network intelligence. The centralized and separated operations enable organizations to have greater agility to manage, monitor, deploy, expand, automate, and troubleshoot the network.
See More: Top 10 Network Access Control Software Solutions in 2021

Types of Network Software

There are numerous types of network software available, with most of them being categorized under the communications and security arena. The varieties of network software differ based on their key features and costs. The main role of network software is to eliminate the dependence on hardware by streamlining communications across multiple devices, locations, and systems. Not only are they extremely useful for end-user hardware (laptops, desktops), the addition of software is bound to have a positive effect on the organization's everyday functioning and operations.

1. Network storage software

In many ways, data within networks is like a child. With time, it only grows, and as it does, it requires adequate attention. Soon enough, data needs to be stored spanning multiple locations and a wide range of devices. Network storage software allows businesses to utilize a standard interface that manages countless databases between users or clients. It serves as a good manager of access between various departments or essential communities within an organization. This way, anybody having access can view or retrieve information with just a click, and at the same time, security concerns are also taken care of.

2. Data archiving software

In today's day and age of dynamic networks spread across various functioning corporate entities, data once misplaced is data lost. Hence, it is vital to take regular backups. As organizations grow and networks evolve in size, it gets especially tricky to save data appropriately. In addition to that, data that needs to be stored increases at a rapid pace, and its management gets costlier. In such a situation, data archiving software is a perfect choice.

Organizations have heaps of data that might not have to be utilized daily but is still essential to be stored for various purposes, one of them being for regular compliance. Data archiving software enables better management of such information and is an optimal solution to reduce costs while ensuring that the data is being protected. However, as a word of caution, archive software does not function the same way as regular standard backups. Hence, it is always recommended to ensure that the archived data doesn't need to be accessed soon.

3. Patch management software

It is a nightmare for IT employees to install updates on each device individually. Moreover, when a network consists of numerous devices, ensuring the timely installation of updates is not only expensive but often a cumbersome process as well. As the name suggests, patch management software aids in the smoother management of updates across numerous devices on the network through the installation of patches. This makes the process more seamless and enables each machine to download a patch managed by central software and run updates automatically. Patch management software is the more hassle-free and effective way to perform continuous updates across devices and systems in an organization.

4. Security surveillance software

A majority of network software focuses on data storage and linking devices. However, they do not incorporate protection for a network. This is where security surveillance software comes into the picture. It monitors and connects the various security solutions within a network. Specific software is ideal for large networks as it effortlessly links throughout locations and provides credible browser-based live and recorded footage to an organization.

On the other hand, better-targeted software works well in protecting vulnerable units by building a network architecture that reduces attack surfaces, thereby keeping components hidden from any malicious parties. This happens through developing outbound-only connections with cloud services and providers.

5. Asset management software

One of the most challenging tasks in any organization is to keep the network up and running efficiently. Achieving this demands greater visibility of the network infrastructure as well as regular tracking and monitoring of essential metrics. That's where asset management software comes to the rescue.

Compared to most of its counterparts, asset management software operates from a centralized server room or hub and is not connected to any hardware. This is good in terms of cost reduction and offers an excellent experience to the users and clients.

6. Deployment and migration software

Managing a network comes with regular upgrades or movement of assets, and this can sometimes become a herculean task. However, it doesn't have to be so. The use of deployment and migration software aids organizations in making processes such as upgrading systems hassle-free. The software provides an interface that enables easy monitoring of any deployment or data movement between the hardware and databases within the network. It also ensures mandatory checks on compatibility when any data is being moved between regular backups and archives, thereby significantly reducing the chances of data loss.

7. Printer and fax software

Printers and fax machines are indispensable equipment for any working organization. As an organization grows, so does the number of assets involved within its network. Standard options such as Wi-Fi printing might not always be the best choice, especially for big corporations or schools that span across many floors. This software provides an easy-to-use interface that enables the undertaking and maintenance of multiple tasks. That's not it! With this software, one can easily set IP printing across networks or even deploy updates. What's more? In some cases, it can also enable organizations to fax or print important documents and correspondence across different locations.

8. Network management software

In a sea of countless options, why should an organization opt for network management software? The reason is quite apparent. Their primary function is to monitor, manage, and troubleshoot any hurdles in network performance across the whole device infrastructure. While a network monitoring software might have some basic options plugged in to troubleshoot, network management software is equipped to manipulate and modify network performance for the better. These software applications are hosted by several industry-leading brands.

See More: What Is a Virtual Private Network (VPN)? Definition, Components, Types, Functions, and Best Practices

Top 8 Network Software Management Best Practices for 2022

Network software helps a business become more agile and scale its operations while enabling a more secure and centralized data center. The adoption of network software has grown by leaps and bounds across organizations looking to deploy extremely flexible network infrastructure. Despite its rising popularity, its security and management can take a toll on the operations and network teams. For this, organizations need to follow certain best practices to champion the migration, management, deployment, and security of their network software.

1. Start by asking the right questions

Before taking the big leap, it's best to start by asking important questions. Will your organization benefit from network software solutions? What are its benefits and the challenges that come along? Think about its application based on your organization and sector (IT, healthcare, manufacturing, finance, etc.). Will its migration, integration, and operations affect individual departments in an organization? Whether or not the cost of its updates will be worth the investment and have real merits for customers.

2. Educate your employees

Once you have the answers to the above questions, the next course of action would be to provide the necessary training and support to educate employees, especially key IT personnel, administrators, and operation engineers about the network's architecture, design, and interfaces, to be well prepared for a successful migration. It's also important to perform skill assessment and check for knowledge gaps when it comes to the understanding of the control plane and data plane.

3. Plan the pre-migration phase

Correctly charting the pre-migration stage to the T is crucial when transitioning to any new type of network. In this stage, organizations work to understand business application networks, their flows, and dependencies to make a seamless switch to a new network environment. What typically throws organizations off their course are complex network challenges such as network outages and data flow, scale, and performance problems. Hence, it's essential to plan every step of the move to have the least disruptive transition possible.

4. Know your existing network well

Before proceeding with any type of network migration, it's important to have a detailed understanding of your existing network, especially when functioning with legacy systems and complicated data structures. What might help here is going through similar industry use cases to get a glimpse of real-life challenges surrounding the network architecture, tools, processes, and dependencies that are likely to determine any network impacts.

5. Consider necessary security implications

Lack of a detailed security strategy can bring an organization to its knees. While the centralization of controls may be the best thing for network administrators, it can also offer a single point of opening for a complete network failure, attacks due to uncontrolled traffic, or the risk of malicious content sweeping through. Security measures such as data packet routing through a single firewall and segmentation are a few examples of extremely competent strategies that one could consider.

6. Develop a robust security management policy

Once you have a security strategy in place, the next step is to develop and implement an ongoing security management policy. The ever-so-dynamic nature of business applications requires administrators to modify network policies and keep track of risk and compliance reporting. It's necessary to keep in mind that the system must have the capacity to support both SDN firewalls alongside traditional firewalls. An ideal way to handle the security management policy is to adopt an all-around automated security approach.

7. Start small, then build up

To quickly gain the security benefits of enterprise network management, migrating an entire organization's network software in one go wouldn't be a smart move. Not only would that be risky but also quite challenging. Hence, organizations are advised to start small, plan and document processes, and take a step-by-step approach to mitigate risks. Once this is done, it can be followed by utilizing additional software providing application optimization and other integrations as and when required.

8. Think of post-migration processes

No matter what, the best thing one can do is always stay prepared for any outcome, be it positive or negative. Start by setting metrics and processes to analyze the post-migration results and validate the target network. It's imperative to have a backup plan with older log entries if, in case, there arises the need to go back to the previous working configuration. Network emulation and simulation tools are also particularly beneficial to foresee network behavior before real-life deployment.

What Is Network Hardware?

Network hardware is a set of physical or network devices that are essential for interaction and communication between hardware units operational on a computer network. These are dedicated hardware components that connect to each other and enable a network to function effectively and efficiently.

Today, technology has penetrated its tentacles into every nook and corner of our lives. It has gone from being just an industry add-on to an inevitable necessity. As tech enablement is driving the industrial transformation, it's important for businesses to build a network that is secure, reliable and keeps the users in touch with their applications. The core of this very foundation is leveraged by the basic network hardware.

Network hardware plays a key role as industries grow as it supports scalability. It integrates any number of components depending on the enterprise's needs. Network hardware helps establish an effective mode of communication, thereby improving the business standards. It also promotes multiprocessing and enables sharing of resources, information, and software with ease.

Network equipment is part of advancements of the Ethernet network protocol and utilizes a twisted pair or fiber cable as a connection medium. Routers, hubs, switches, and bridges are some examples of network hardware.

Let's look at the fundamental devices of a computer network.

Modems: A modem enables a computer to connect to the internet via a telephone line. The modem at one end converts the computer's digital signals into analog signals and sends them through a telephone line. At the other end, it converts the analog signals to digital signals that are understandable for another computer.

Routers: A router connects two or more networks. One common use of the router is to connect a home or office network (LAN) to the internet (WAN). It generally has a plugged-in internet cable along with cables that connect computers on the LAN. Alternatively, a LAN connection can also be wireless (Wi-Fi-enabled), making the network device wireless. These are also referred to as wireless access points (WAPs).

Hubs, bridges, and switches: Hubs, bridges, and switches are connecting units that allow multiple devices to connect to the router and enable data transfer to all devices on a network. A router is a complex device with the capabilities of hubs, bridges, and even switches.

Hubs: A hub broadcasts data to all devices on a network. As a result, it consumes a lot of bandwidth as many computers might not need to receive the broadcasted data. The hub could be useful in linking a few gaming consoles in a local multiplayer game via a wired or wireless LAN.

Bridges: A bridge connects two separate LAN networks. It scans for the receiving device before sending a message. This implies that it avoids unnecessary data transfers if the receiving device is not there. Moreover, it also checks to see whether the receiving device has already received the message. These practices improve the overall performance of the network.

Switches: A switch is more powerful than a hub or a bridge but performs a similar role. It stores the MAC addresses of network devices and transfers data packets only to those devices that have requested Thus, when the demand is high, a switch becomes more efficient as it reduces the amount of latency.

Network interface cards: A network interface card (NIC) is a hardware unit installed on a computer, which allows it to connect to a network. It is typically in the form of a circuit board or chip. In most modern machines, NICs are built into the motherboards, while in some computers, an extra expansion card in the form of a small circuit board is added externally.

Network cables: Cables connect different devices on a network. Today, most networks have cables over a wireless connection as they are more secure, i.e., less prone to attacks, and at the same time carry larger volumes of data per second.

Firewall: A firewall is a hardware or software device between a computer and the rest of the network open to attackers or hackers. Thus, a LAN can be protected from hackers by placing a firewall between the LAN and the internet connection. A firewall allows authorized connections and data-like emails or web pages to pass through but blocks unauthorized connections made to a computer or LAN.

See More: What Is Network Security? Definition, Types, and Best Practices

Network Architecture: Key Components

Network architecture defines the structural and logical design of a network. It constitutes hardware devices, physical connections, software, wireless networks, protocols, and transmission media. It gives a detailed overview of the whole network, which organizations use to create LAN, WAN, and other specific communication tunnels.

Network architecture can be viewed from different vantage points depending on the size and purpose of the network. WAN refers to a group of interconnected networks distributed over large distances, while LAN refers to a computer network that interconnects computers within a limited space. Therefore, the architecture of a WAN will vary from that of a LAN in a small office.

Setting up the layout of the network architecture is critical, as it can either enhance or hamper the overall performance of the entire system. For example, selecting inappropriate transmission media or equipment for an expected server load in a network can cause slowdowns in different parts of the network.

As more user devices connect to the network, network architecture becomes even more significant by adding a security layer to protect connected devices. Additionally, modern network architectures support advanced user recognition and authorization.

Most network architectures are built on the open systems interconnection (OSI) model. Here, network tasks are segregated into seven logical layers, right from the lowest to the highest abstraction. For example, the lowest physical layer manages the wire and cable connections of the network, while the highest application layer deals with APIs that perform application-specific functions such as chat or file sharing. Overall, with the OSI model, troubleshooting the network is easier as the problems are isolated from each other at different layers.

Network architecture design is more about optimizing its fundamental building blocks. These include four key components:

1. Hardware

Hardware refers to network devices that form the core of any network. These include user devices (laptops, PDAs, mobile phones), routers, servers, and gateways. The basic objective of any network architecture is to establish an efficient mechanism to transfer data from one hardware device to another.

2. Transmission media

Transmission media encompasses all physical connections between network (hardware) devices. The properties of different transmission media determine the speed of data transfer from one endpoint to another. These can be wired and wireless. Wired media include physical wires or cables used for connections within a network, such as coaxial or fiber optics. On the other hand, wireless media operates on properties of microwave or radio signals, such as Wi-Fi or cellular.

3. Protocols

Protocols refer to the rules that govern data movement between network devices. Various machines on a network communicate with each other using this common protocol language. Without these protocols in place, it would be difficult for your iPhone to access a web page that is essentially stored on a Linux server.

The nature of data decides the type of network protocol it needs to adopt. For example, transmission control protocol/internet protocol (TCP/IP) is used to connect to the internet, while file transfer protocol (FTP) is used for sending and receiving files to and from a server. Similarly, Ethernet protocol is used for connecting one computing device to another.

4. Topology

Network topology defines how the network is wired together and highlights the network's structure. This is important because variables such as distance between communicating devices can impact its data transfer speed, thereby affecting overall network performance.

Several topologies exist, each with specific strengths and weaknesses. For example, consider a star topology. In this case, all the network devices are connected to a central hub. The strength of this topology is such that any device can connect to the network easily. However, in situations when the central hub fails, the whole network can crash almost instantly.

Another topology is that of a bus, where all devices are connected along a single pathway, termed as a bus. The bus resembles a highway that transports data from one endpoint to another. Although this topology is easy and affordable to implement, its performance can take a hit as more devices get added to the network.

Today, most network architectures adopt a hybrid approach where different topologies are combined and blended to compensate for each one's weakness.

See More: Wide Area Network (WAN) vs. Local Area Network (LAN): Key Differences and Similarities

8 Challenges of Network Hardware Today

Addressing common hardware issues such as overloaded servers or overheated equipment is crucial for any business to flourish. Failing to do so can cause substantial revenue loss or hamper business growth through unexpected customer attrition.

According to a recent Infrascale survey of 500 C-level executives at SMBs, hardware failures are the reason for 38% of network downtime. This creates inevitable business challenges for several SMBs. Hence, it is important to have a system that monitors the hardware 24/7. Although hardware failure can occur due to several factors, here are some of the main challenges of network hardware.

1. Physical connectivity challenges

Defective cables and connectors on a network can generate errors on the network devices to which they are connected. The problem aggravates due to a broken or malfunctioning cable. The issue can even crop up on the outside of the LAN infrastructure. Damage to a copper cable or fiber optic connector can significantly reduce the volume of data it can transfer. It can also lead to considerable packet loss.

This challenge can be overcome by adopting a network performance monitoring software that monitors the network for defective cables or connectors. It can also aid in measuring errors on all network interfaces and trigger alerts as and when problems are identified.

2. Malfunctioning hardware devices

Network issues can arise due to malfunctioning network equipment, including firewalls, routers, switches, and wireless access points. The possible reasons for this could be bad configurations, faulty connections, or even disabled devices. It is essential to ensure that all the devices on the network are configured appropriately, as misconfiguration issues can affect different parts of the network, thereby impacting its performance. Such a challenge can be countered by paying close attention to all the devices and switches to verify if they are working normally.

3. DNS issues

Domain name system (DNS) is analogous to a directory for the internet, and every internet-connected device matches domain names with the IP addresses of the websites. Computers can connect to other devices via the internet and look up websites through their IP addresses. As you enter the domain name in a web browser, the DNS finds the content connected to that domain.

DNS problems are common in most networks and can be caused due to hardware failure on the host machine or network. Such challenges can be addressed by troubleshooting network/ hardware configuration settings via network performance monitoring software. This helps in identifying problems at their source.

4. Temperature issues

Most hardware failures occur due to an abnormal spike in temperature. Abnormal heating or cooling in network units can cause the abrupt shutting down or freezing of hardware systems, which eventually results in their failure. As network devices compute large quantities of data, the optimal temperature needs to be maintained to function efficiently.

5. Ventilation problems

As the temperature of the network equipment rises, the performance and speed of its operation slow down. It can even break down in some cases. Poor ventilation arising due to inappropriate device arrangement or wrongful fan setup may not be able to tackle or handle the extra heat produced by network devices. This can worsen and have an adverse effect on network productivity.

6. Overutilization of capacity

Exploiting the surplus capacity of network equipment can slow it down considerably, thereby leading to performance lag. This is one of the prominent network hardware challenges where devices with limited computing resources are overburdened with the excess workload. Such challenges can be tackled by controlling the overutilization of device capacity by resorting to workload division and distribution among other network devices.

7. Fluctuation in power supply

Corroded cable connections or other external factors can lead to notable fluctuations in power supply. In some cases, there can be a sudden surge in power supply, which can cause unplanned outages. Such events can lead to short circuits that can impact the performance of an individual device or the entire network.

8. Battery overuse

The efficiency of a battery takes a hit once 80% of its energy is utilized. Draining the battery can cause cache data loss or a sudden device or server shutdown. Moreover, low-capacity batteries lack power efficiency and have a short shelf life. Such battery units can affect the overall capability of the device and, in turn, affect the entire network.

See More: What Is a Content Delivery Network (CDN)? Definition, Architecture, and Best Practices

Top 10 Best Practices of Network Hardware Management for 2022
Proper network hardware management can help address various hardware challenges. It can ensure that the network infrastructure is secure and not susceptible to device hardware failures. Let's look at the top 10 practices to leverage better hardware management and establish efficient network operations. The practices listed below provide solutions in addition to addressing the hardware challenges that have been discussed above.

1. Opt for multi-vendor support

Modern networks comprise heterogeneous approaches to increase their capability compared to traditional homogeneous networks. Along with default vendor-supported systems, businesses are embracing custom-configured devices that provide specific business solutions. Thus, hardware monitoring practices should support multi-vendor devices irrespective of vendor or configuration barriers.

Moreover, technicians resolving network issues need to have complete visibility into multi-vendor hardware devices in real time.

2. Prioritize critical alerts

Network hardware issues should be prioritized considering two factors: the criticality of the device and the significance of the underlying issue. Additionally, hardware problems are managed by several parties spread across teams and even geographies. It is crucial to push the alerts to the right teams through the right channels in such cases. This creates a well-defined fault resolution path that is properly regulated and managed and will help resolve hardware faults faster and in an optimized manner.

3. Proactively monitor and troubleshoot

Instead of resolving hardware problems after an issue occurs, practicing proactive measures to avoid hardware failure in the initial stage can save a lot of time and resources. Technicians should be alerted in advance based on preemptive hardware device monitoring and management. This will ensure that issues are addressed before they worsen and damage the organizational network.

This practice can be enabled by utilizing historic performance reports to predict and forecast untimely hardware failure. The method of proactive monitoring and troubleshooting ensures that issues are taken care of well in advance.

4. Gain deeper visibility

Hardware issues require an in-depth understanding of the root cause of the problem to resolve them without impacting the network's overall performance. Hence, one has to gain deeper visibility into the performance of hardware devices to address the minutest problems. Technicians can easily diagnose and fix issues in network hardware devices if they have access to the tiniest details of the hardware devices. This not only improves hardware efficiency but ensures that the network is not affected by hardware problems.

5. Automate basic tasks

L1/L2 troubleshooting operations and fundamental maintenance tasks are quite repetitive. These are time- and resource-consuming activities. As such, automating such tasks can give technicians the liberty and more time to focus on critical hardware alerts that require immediate remedial action. Moreover, technicians also need to keep a tab on the interruptions or failures that may occur in these automated tasks. In simple words, a healthy blend of manual and automation can help in resolving hardware issues quickly.

6. Ensure clarity on hardware dependencies & processes

Failure in one hardware device implies that another device dependent on it will face significant performance degradation. In some cases, it may even lead to the failure of a series of hardware devices. Thus, to prevent total network outage, it is vital to keep track of connectivity along all the hardware devices in the network.

Internal processes and applications can also sometimes cause hardware failures. Hence, having an effective process and application management system in place can ensure that performance slowdown does not result in hardware failure at any point in time.

7. Troubleshoot cable connectivity issues

The cables used for network connections differ depending on the required connectivity type. For example, connectivity between a router and a computer is enabled with a crossover cable. Hence, it is crucial to ensure that a suitable cable is used to make a physical connection between any two network devices.

If the connections are fine, you can conclude that the cable is faulty. This can be verified by replacing the existing cable with a newer one and checking the connectivity. If the problem persists, the port or interface on which the link is terminated needs to be checked, as there is a slim chance that the port may be faulty.

8. Handle faulty ports

In a faulty port scenario, one needs to check that the port or interface on which the link is established is not off or shut down. Verifying the duplex mode and data transfer speed can also help. Additionally, when the port is running fine, but still the problem exists, you can check the indicator lights on each device.

The lights show the running status of the port, i.e., whether the port is physically radiating or not functioning. The physically malfunctioning port will be evident from the light status. It is recommended to configure the link on any other free port or interface in such cases.

9. Verify traffic overload

In situations where there is more traffic than the carrying capacity at a link or interface, it may start behaving abnormally. Thus it is vital to verify traffic overload at a link or interface by inspecting the volume of data packets at a given time on the link under consideration. This ensures the smooth running of hardware devices on the network.

10. Troubleshoot routing problems

While routing data packets on a network, the possibility of fault occurrence is high. Hence, plans for resolving issues can be laid down depending on the fault type. Floating data packets from source to destination hosts can become rogue if the wrong routing protocol is used to find the route to the next hop.

Another issue can relate to malfunctioning firewalls or routing devices. In one scenario, the firewall may prevent the entry of data packets to the destination. In another case, configuration faults at the router end can cause problems for the movement of data packets in a network. Therefore, it is important to troubleshoot concerned routing devices to allow the seamless movement of data packets.

COMPUTER SHORTCUT KEYS

Computer shortcut keys, from A to Z (Basic)

The most basic and often performed computer tasks are text selection, copying, pasting, and deleting. Instead of using your pointer, you should be comfortable with keyboard shortcuts. The table below contains all of the common keyboard shortcuts for computers that should be used frequently. Learn about every basic computer shortcut key from A to Z in the table below.

Basic Computer Shortcut Keys A to Z	
Shortcuts	**Uses of Shortcut keys**
Alt + F	File menu options in the current program
Alt + E	Edits options in the current program
F1	Universal help (for any sort of program)
Ctrl + A	Selects all text
Ctrl + X	Cuts the selected item
Ctrl + Del	Cut selected item
Ctrl + C	Copy the selected item
Ctrl + Ins	Copy the selected item
Ctrl + V	Paste the selected item
Shift + Ins	Paste the selected item
Home	Takes the user to the start of the current line
Ctrl + Home	Go to the beginning of the document
End	Go to the end of the current line
Ctrl + End	Go to the end of a document
Shift + Home	Highlight from the prevailing position to the start of the line
Shift + End	Highlight from the prevailing position to the end of the line
Ctrl + (Left arrow)	Move one term to the left at a time
Ctrl + (Right arrow)	Move one term to the right at a time

Computer shortcuts are keys or key combinations that allow you to complete things faster than you would with a mouse or cursor. All of Microsoft Windows' keyboard shortcuts are shown below. Let's have a look at the Microsoft Windows keyboard shortcuts in the table below.

shortcut Keys	**Uses of Shortcut keys**
Ctrl + Plus Key	Adjust the widths of all columns automatically, in Windows Explorer
Alt + Enter	Open the properties window for the selected icon or program
Alt + Print Screen	Take a screenshot of the current page.
Ctrl + Alt + Del	Reboot/Windows task manager
Ctrl + Esc	These keys allow you to activate the start menu
F4	Its purpose in Windows 95 to XP is to open the located window
F5	Refresh the contents of your windows system
F3	Find anything from your system's desktop
Alt + Esc	Switch between desktop applications on the taskbar
F2	Rename the selected icon
Alt + Shift + Tab	It allows you to switch back between ongoing applications
Alt + Tab	Switch between open applications/ programs.
Shift + Delete	When you press the Shift and Delete keys together, your program or files will be deleted permanently.
Alt + F4	It is used to close the ongoing program
Ctrl + F4	It's used to swiftly close a document or a file that's currently open.

More shortcut keys

- Copy: Ctrl + C
- Cut: Ctrl + X
- Paste: Ctrl + V
- Maximize Window: F11 or Windows logo key + Up arrow
- Open Task View: Windows logo key + Tab
- Display and hide the desktop: Windows logo key + D
- Switch between open apps: Alt + Tab
- Open the Quick Link menu: Windows logo key + X
- Lock your PC: Windows logo key + L

Keyboard shortcuts for Microsoft Excel

If you are unfamiliar with the shortcut keys for MS Excel, creating a large spreadsheet and then altering the data or any one piece of information inside the entire sheet will take time. Below is a discussion of all the computer shortcut keys for Microsoft Office applications. To learn about the shortcut keys used in MS Excel, see the table below.

Shortcut keys	**Uses of shortcut keys**
Alt + Shift + F1	When you wanna insert new worksheet use these keys together
Shift + F3	With the help of these keys, you can open the MS-Excel formula window
Shift + F5	When you press these keys together it will open the search box
F11	The F11 key is used to create a chart in MS-Excel
Ctrl + Shift +;	With the help of these keys, you can enter the current time
Ctrl +;	Use these keys together to enter the current date
Ctrl + K	When you want to Insert a link, you can use these keys together
Ctrl + F	These keys are used to open find and replace options in MS-Excel
Ctrl + G	Use these keys together to open go-to options

Ctrl + B	When you press these keys together it will bold highlighted selection.
F2	When you want to edit the selected cell using this key
F5	With the help of this key, you can go to a specific cell
F7	With the help of this key, you can check the spell of selected text
Ctrl + I	These commands are used to Italicize highlighted selection.
Ctrl + Space	Use these keys together to select the entire column
Shift + Space	Use these keys together to select the entire row
Ctrl + W	Use these keys together to close the document
Ctrl + H	Use these keys to open find and replace options
Ctrl + U	With help of these keys, you can underline highlighted text.
Ctrl + Y	With help of these keys, you can underline highlighted text.
Ctrl + Z	With the help of these keys, you can undo the last deleted action
Ctrl + F9	Use these keys to minimize a current window in MS-Excel
Ctrl + F10	Use these keys to maximize the currently selected window in MS-Excel
Ctrl + Tab	With the help of these keys, you can move between two or more open MS-Excel files
Alt + =	With the help of these keys, you can initiate the formula to add all of the above cells
Ctrl +	With the use of these keys together you can insert the value in the current cell from the above cell.
Ctrl + (Right arrow)	With the help of these keys, you can jump on to the next section of text
Ctrl + O	Use these keys to open options in MS-Excel
Ctrl + N	Use these keys together to open the document in MS-Excel

Ctrl + P	Use these keys together to open the print dialogue box in MS-Excel

Keyboard shortcuts for Microsoft Word

Despite the fact that MS Word is the most fundamental and appears to be the simplest to use, However, MS Word typing is made simple and fun with a comprehensive list of computer shortcut keys. Below are listed all of the computer shortcut keys connected to Microsoft Word. To learn the shortcut keys used in MS Word, see the table below.

Shortcuts	**Uses of Shortcut keys**
Ctrl + B	Bold highlighted selection
Ctrl + C	Copy selected text
Ctrl + X	Cut selected text
Ctrl + N	Open new/blank document
Ctrl + O	Open options
Ctrl + P	Open the print window
Ctrl + F	Open find box
Ctrl + I	Italicize highlighted selection
Ctrl + K	Insert link
Ctrl + U	Underline highlighted selection
Ctrl + V	Paste
Ctrl + G	Find and replace options
Ctrl + H	Find and replace options
Ctrl + J	Justify paragraph alignment
Ctrl + L	Align selected text or line to the left

Ctrl + Q	Align the selected paragraph to the left
Ctrl + E	Align selected text or line to the centre
Ctrl + R	Align selected text or line to the right
Ctrl + M	Indent the paragraph
Ctrl + T	Hanging indent
Ctrl + D	Font options
Ctrl + Shift + F	Change the font
Ctrl + Shift + >	Increase selected font +1
Ctrl +]	Increase selected font +1
Ctrl + [	Decrease selected font -1
Ctrl + Shift + *	View or hide non-printing characters
Ctrl + (Left arrow)	Move one word to the left
Ctrl + (Right arrow)	Move one word to the right
Ctrl + (Up arrow)	Move to the beginning of the line or paragraph
Ctrl + (Down arrow)	Move to the end of the paragraph
Ctrl + Del	Delete the word to the right of the cursor
Ctrl + Backspace	Delete the word to the left of the cursor
Ctrl + End	Move the cursor to the end of the document
Ctrl + Home	Move the cursor to the beginning of the document
Ctrl + Space	Reset highlighted text to the default font
Ctrl + 1	Single-space lines
Ctrl + 2	Double-space lines
Ctrl + 5	1.5-line spacing
Ctrl + Alt + 1	Change text to heading 1

Ctrl + Alt + 2	Change text to heading 2
Ctrl + Alt + 3	Change text to heading 3
Shift + F3	Change the case of the selected text
Shift + Insert	Paste
F4	Repeat the last action performed (Word 2000+)
F7	Spell-check selected text and/or document
Shift + F7	Activate the thesaurus
F12	Save as
Ctrl + S	Save
Shift + F12	Save
Alt + Shift + D	Insert the current date
Alt + Shift + T	Insert the current time
Ctrl + W	Close document
Ctrl+=	Set chosen text as a subscript.
Ctrl+Shift+=	Set chosen text as superscript.

PowerPoint shortcuts on the computer

Look at the computer shortcut keys used in the PowerPoint application if you're just starting to work with Microsoft Powerpoint and want to understand how to browse and execute commands quickly. Below are listed all of the computer shortcut keys for PowerPoint programmes.

Shortcuts Keys	**Uses of Shortcut Keys**
Ctrl+Shift+<	Reduce the font size of the selected text by one size.
CTRL + G	Group things together

Ctrl+M	Create a new slide just after your chosen slide.
CTRL + D	Create a duplicate of your current slide.
Esc	Exit the ongoing slide show and it will redirect you to the earlier live view.
Ctrl+K	When you want to enter a hyperlink use these keys together.
Ctrl+Shift+>	These commands are used to maximize the font size of the selected text by one size.
F5	With the help of F5, you can start the presentation from the initial slide.
Ctrl+N	These commands are used in a different Powerpoint software window, create a new, blank slide.

What are the 20 shortcut keys?

Basic Windows keyboard shortcuts

- Ctrl+W: Close.
- Ctrl+A: Select all.
- Alt+Tab: Switch apps.
- Alt+F4: Close apps.
- Win+D: Show or hide the desktop.
- Win+left arrow or Win+right arrow: Snap windows.
- Win+Tab: Open the Task view.
- Tab and Shift+Tab: Move backwards and forward through options. etc

Microsoft Office

Microsoft Office, or simply **Office**, is a discontinued family of client software, server software, and services developed by Microsoft. It was first announced by Bill Gates on August 1, 1988, at COMDEX in Las Vegas. Initially a marketing term for an office suite (bundled set of productivity applications), the first version of Office contained Microsoft Word, Microsoft Excel, and Microsoft PowerPoint. Over the years, Office applications have grown substantially closer with shared features such as a common spell checker, Object Linking and Embedding data integration and Visual Basic for Applications scripting language. Microsoft also positions Office as a development platform for line-of-business software under the Office Business Applications brand.

It contains a word processor (Word), a spreadsheet program (Excel) and a presentation program (PowerPoint), an email client (Outlook), a database management system (Access), and a desktop publishing app (Publisher).

Office is produced in several versions targeted towards different end-users and computing environments. The original, and most widely used version, is the desktop version, available for PCs running the Windows and macOS operating systems. Microsoft also maintains mobile apps for Android and iOS. Office on the web is a version of the software that runs within a web browser.

Since Office 2013, Microsoft has promoted Office 365 as the primary means of obtaining Microsoft Office: it allows the use of the software and other services on a subscription business model, and users receive feature updates to the software for the lifetime of the subscription, including new features and cloud computing integration that are not necessarily included in the "on-premises" releases of Office sold under conventional license terms. In 2017, revenue from Office 365 overtook conventional license sales. Microsoft also rebranded most of their standard Office 365 editions as "Microsoft 365" to reflect their inclusion of features and services beyond the core Microsoft Office suite.

In October 2022, Microsoft announced that it will phase out the Microsoft Office brand in favor of "Microsoft 365" by January 2023. The name will continue to be used for legacy product offerings.

Core apps and services

Microsoft Word is a word processor included in Microsoft Office and some editions of the now-discontinued Microsoft Works. The first version of Word, released in the autumn of 1983, was for the MS-DOS operating system and introduced the computer mouse to more users. Word 1.0 could be purchased with a bundled mouse, though none was required. Following the precedents of LisaWrite and MacWrite, Word for Macintosh attempted to add closer WYSIWYG features into its package. Word for Mac was released in 1985.

Word for Mac was the first graphical version of Microsoft Word. Initially, it implemented the proprietary .doc format as its primary format. Word 2007, however, deprecated this format in favor of Office Open XML, which was later standardized by Ecma International as an open format. Support for Portable Document Format (PDF) and OpenDocument (ODF) was first introduced in Word for Windows with Service Pack 2 for Word 2007.

Microsoft Excel is a spreadsheet editor that originally competed with the dominant Lotus 1-2-3 and eventually outsold it. Microsoft released the first version of Excel for the Mac OS in 1985 and the first Windows version (numbered 2.05 to line up with the Mac) in November 1987.

Microsoft PowerPoint is a presentation program used to create slideshows composed of text, graphics, and other objects, which can be displayed on-screen and shown by the presenter or printed out on transparencies or slides.

Microsoft OneNote is a notetaking program that gathers handwritten or typed notes, drawings, screen clippings and audio commentaries. Notes can be shared with other OneNote users over the Internet or a network. OneNote was initially introduced as a standalone app that was not included in any Microsoft Office 2003 edition. However, OneNote eventually became a core component of Microsoft Office; with the release of Microsoft Office 2013, OneNote was included in all Microsoft Office offerings. OneNote is also available as a web app on Office on the web, a freemium (and later freeware) Windows desktop app, a mobile app for Windows Phone, iOS, Android, and Symbian, and a Metro-style app for Windows 8 or later.

Microsoft Outlook (not to be confused with Outlook Express, Outlook.com or Outlook on the web) is a personal information manager that replaces Windows Messaging, Microsoft Mail, and Schedule+ starting in Office 97; it includes an e-mail client, calendar, task manager and address book. On the Mac OS, Microsoft offered several versions of Outlook in the late 1990s, but only for use with Microsoft Exchange Server. In Office 2001, it introduced an alternative application with a slightly different feature set called Microsoft Entourage. It reintroduced Outlook in Office 2011, replacing Entourage.

Microsoft OneDrive is a file hosting service that allows users to sync files and later access them from a web browser or mobile device.

Microsoft Teams is a platform that combines workplace chat, meetings, notes, and attachments.

Windows-only apps

Microsoft Publisher is a desktop publishing app for Windows mostly used for designing brochures, labels, calendars, greeting cards, business cards, newsletters, web sites, and postcards.

Microsoft Access is a database management system for Windows that combines the relational Access Database Engine (formerly Jet Database Engine) with a graphical user interface and software development tools. Microsoft Access stores data in its own format based on the Access Database Engine. It can also import or link directly to data stored in other applications and databases.

Microsoft Project is a project management app for Windows to keep track of events and to create network charts and Gantt charts, not bundled in any Office suite.

Microsoft Visio is a diagram and flowcharting app for Windows not bundled in any Office suite.

Mobile-only apps

Office Lens is an image scanner optimized for mobile devices. It captures the document (e.g. business card, paper, whiteboard) via the camera and then straightens the document portion of the image. The result can be exported to Word, OneNote, PowerPoint or Outlook, or saved in OneDrive, sent via Mail or placed in Photo Library.

Office Mobile is a unified Office mobile app for Android and iOS, which combines Word, Excel, and PowerPoint into a single app and introduces new capabilities as making quick notes, signing PDFs, scanning QR codes, and transferring files.

Office Remote is an application that turns the mobile device into a remote control for desktop versions of Word, Excel and PowerPoint.

Server applications

Microsoft SharePoint is a web-based collaborative platform that integrates with Microsoft Office. Launched in 2001, SharePoint is primarily sold as a document management and storage system, but the product is highly configurable and usage varies substantially among organizations. SharePoint services include:

- Excel Services is a spreadsheet editing server similar to Microsoft Excel.
- InfoPath Forms Services is a form distribution server similar to Microsoft InfoPath.
- Microsoft Project Server is a project management server similar to Microsoft Project.
- Microsoft Search Server

Skype for Business Server is a real-time communications server for instant messaging and video-conferencing.

Microsoft Exchange Server is a mail server and calendaring server.

Web services

- **Microsoft Sway** is a presentation web app released in October 2014. It also has a native app for iOS and Windows 10.
- **Delve** is a service that allows Office 365 users to search and manage their emails, meetings, contacts, social networks and documents stored on OneDrive or Sites in Office 365.

- **Microsoft Forms** is an online survey creator, available for Office 365 Education subscribers.
- **Microsoft To Do** is a task management service.
- **Outlook.com** is a free webmail with a user interface similar to Microsoft Outlook.
- **Outlook on the web** is a webmail client similar to Outlook.com but more comprehensive and available only through Office 365 and Microsoft Exchange Server offerings.
- **Microsoft Planner** is a planning application available on the Microsoft Office 365 platform.
- **Microsoft Stream** is a corporate video sharing service for enterprise users with an Office 365 Academic or Enterprise license.
- **Microsoft Bookings** is an appointment booking application on the Microsoft Office 365 platform.

Office on the web

Office on the web is a free lightweight web version of Microsoft Office and primarily includes three web applications: Word, Excel and PowerPoint. The offering also includes Outlook.com, OneNote and OneDrive which are accessible through a unified app switcher. Users can install the on-premises version of this service, called Office Online Server, in private clouds in conjunction with SharePoint, Microsoft Exchange Server and Microsoft Lync Server.

Word, Excel, and PowerPoint on the web can all natively open, edit, and save Office Open XML files (docx, xlsx, pptx) as well as OpenDocument files (odt, ods, odp). They can also open the older Office file formats (doc, xls, ppt), but will be converted to the newer Open XML formats if the user wishes to edit them online. Other formats cannot be opened in the browser apps, such as CSV in Excel or HTML in Word, nor can Office files that are encrypted with a password be opened. Files with macros can be opened in the browser apps, but the macros cannot be accessed or executed. Starting in July 2013, Word can render PDF documents or convert them to Microsoft Word documents, although the formatting of the document may deviate from the original. Since November 2013, the apps have supported real-time co-authoring and autosaving files.

Office on the web lacks a number of the advanced features present in the full desktop versions of Office, including lacking the programs Access and Publisher entirely. However, users are able to select the command "Open in Desktop App" that brings up the document in the desktop version of Office on their computer or device to utilize the advanced features there.

Supported web browsers include Microsoft Edge, Internet Explorer 11, the latest versions of Firefox or Google Chrome, as well as Safari for OS X 10.8 or later. The Personal edition of Office on the web is available to the general public free of charge with a Microsoft account through the Office.com website, which superseded SkyDrive (now OneDrive) and Office Live Workspace. Enterprise-managed versions are available through Office 365. In February 2013, the ability to view and edit files on SkyDrive without signing in was added. The service can also be installed privately in enterprise environments as a SharePoint app, or through Office Web Apps Server. Microsoft also offers other web apps in the Office suite, such as the Outlook Web App (formerly Outlook Web Access), Lync Web App (formerly Office Communicator Web Access), Project Web App (formerly Project Web Access). Additionally, Microsoft offers a service under the name of Online Doc Viewer to view Office documents on a website via Office on the web.

Common features

Most versions of Microsoft Office (including Office 97 and later) use their own widget set and do not exactly match the native operating system. This is most apparent in Microsoft Office XP and 2003, where the standard menus were replaced with a colored, flat-looking, shadowed menu style.

The user interface of a particular version of Microsoft Office often heavily influences a subsequent version of Microsoft Windows. E.g.:-

The toolbar, colored buttons and the gray-colored 3D look of Office 4.3 were added to Windows 95.

The ribbon, introduced in Office 2007, has been incorporated into several programs bundled with Windows 7 and later.

The flat, box-like design of Office 2013 (released in 2012) was replicated in Windows 8's new UI revamp. Users of Microsoft Office may access external data via connection-specifications saved in Office Data Connection (.odc) files.

Office, on all platforms, support editing both server files (in real time) and offline files (manually saved) in the recent years. The support for editing server files (in real time) was originally introduced (in its current form) after the introduction of OneDrive (formerly SkyDrive). But, older versions of Office also have the ability to edit server files (notably Office 2007).

Both Windows and Office used service packs to update software. Office had non-cumulative service releases, which were discontinued after Office 2000 Service Release 1. Now, Windows and Office have shifted to predictable (monthly, semi-annual and annual) release schemes to update software.

Past versions of Office often contained Easter eggs. For example, Excel 97 contained a reasonably functional flight-simulator.

File formats and metadata

Microsoft Office prior to Office 2007 used proprietary file formats based on the OLE Compound File Binary Format. This forced users who share data to adopt the same software platform. In 2008, Microsoft made the entire documentation for the binary Office formats freely available for download and granted any possible patents rights for use or implementations of those binary format for free under the Open Specification Promise. Previously, Microsoft had supplied such documentation freely but only on request.

Starting with Office 2007, the default file format has been a version of Office Open XML, though different from the one standardized and published by Ecma International and by ISO/IEC. Microsoft has granted patent rights to the formats technology under the Open Specification Promise and has made available free downloadable converters for previous versions of Microsoft Office including Office 2003, Office XP,

Office 2000 and Office 2004 for Mac OS X. Third-party implementations of Office Open XML exist on the Windows platform (LibreOffice, all platforms), macOS platform (iWork '08, NeoOffice, LibreOffice) and Linux (LibreOffice and OpenOffice.org 3.0). In addition, Office 2010, Service Pack 2 for Office 2007, and Office 2016 for Mac supports the OpenDocument Format (ODF) for opening and saving documents – only the old ODF 1.0 (2006 ISO/IEC standard) is supported, not the 1.2 version (2015 ISO/IEC standard).

Microsoft provides the ability to remove metadata from Office documents. This was in response to highly publicized incidents where sensitive data about a document was leaked via its metadata. Metadata removal was first available in 2004, when Microsoft released a tool called Remove Hidden Data Add-in for Office 2003/XP for this purpose. It was directly integrated into Office 2007 in a feature called the Document Inspector.

Extensibility

A major feature of the Office suite is the ability for users and third-party companies to write add-ins (plug-ins) that extend the capabilities of an application by adding custom commands and specialized features. One of the new features is the Office Store. Plugins and other tools can be downloaded by users. Developers can make money by selling their applications in the Office Store. The revenue is divided between the developer and Microsoft where the developer gets 80% of the money. Developers are able to share applications with all Office users.

The app travels with the document, and it is for the developer to decide what the recipient will see when they open it. The recipient will either have the option to download the app from the Office Store for free, start a free trial or be directed to payment. With Office's cloud abilities, IT departments can create a set of apps for their business employees in order to increase their productivity. When employees go to the Office Store, they'll see their company's apps under My Organization. The apps that employees have personally downloaded will appear under My Apps. Developers can use web technologies like HTML5, XML, CSS3, JavaScript, and APIs for building the apps. An application for Office is a webpage that is hosted inside an Office client application. Users can use apps to amplify the functionality of a document, email message, meeting request, or appointment. Apps can run in multiple environments and by multiple clients, including rich Office desktop clients, Office Web Apps, mobile browsers, and also on-premises and in the cloud. The type of add-ins supported differ by Office versions:

- Office 97 onwards (standard Windows DLLs i.e. Word WLLs and Excel XLLs)
- Office 2000 onwards (COM add-ins)[51]
- Office XP onwards (COM/OLE Automation add-ins)[52]
- Office 2003 onwards (Managed code add-ins – VSTO solutions)[53]

Password protection

Microsoft Office has a security feature that allows users to encrypt Office (Word, Excel, PowerPoint, Access, Skype Business) documents with a user-provided password. The password can contain up to 255 characters and uses AES 128-bit advanced encryption by default. Passwords can also be used to restrict modification of the entire document, worksheet or presentation. Due to lack of document encryption, though, these passwords can be removed using a third-party cracking software.

Support policies

Approach

All versions of Microsoft Office products from Office 2000 to Office 2016 are eligible for ten years of support following their release, during which Microsoft releases security updates for the product version and provides paid technical support. The ten-year period is divided into two five-year phases: The mainstream phase and the extended phase.

During the mainstream phase, Microsoft may provide limited complimentary technical support and release non-security updates or change the design of the product. During the extended phase, said services stop. Office 2019 only receives 5 years of mainstream and 2 years of extended support and Office 2021 only gets 5 years of mainstream support.

Timelines of support

Platforms

Microsoft supports Office for the Windows and macOS platforms, as well as mobile versions for Windows Phone, Android and iOS platforms. Beginning with Mac Office 4.2, the macOS and Windows versions of Office share the same file format, and are interoperable. Visual Basic for Applications support was dropped in Microsoft Office 2008 for Mac, then reintroduced in Office for Mac 2011.

Microsoft tried in the mid-1990s to port Office to RISC processors such as NEC/MIPS and IBM/PowerPC, but they met problems such as memory access being hampered by data structure alignment requirements. Microsoft Word 97 and Excel 97, however, did ship for the DEC Alpha platform. Difficulties in porting Office may have been a factor in discontinuing Windows NT on non-Intel platforms.

Pricing model and editions

The Microsoft Office applications and suites are sold via retail channels, and volume licensing for larger organizations (also including the "Home Use Program". allowing users at participating organizations to buy low-cost licenses for use on their personal devices as part of their employer's volume license agreement).

In 2010, Microsoft introduced a software as a service platform known as Office 365, to provide cloud-hosted versions of Office's server software, including Exchange e-mail and SharePoint, on a subscription basis (competing in particular with Google Apps). Following the release of Office 2013, Microsoft began to offer Office 365 plans for the consumer market, with access to Microsoft Office software on multiple devices with free feature updates over the life of the subscription, as well as other services such as OneDrive storage.

Microsoft has since promoted Office 365 as the primary means of purchasing Microsoft Office. Although there are still "on-premises" releases roughly every three years, Microsoft marketing emphasizes that they do not receive new features or access to new cloud-based services as they are released unlike Office 365, as well as other benefits for consumer and business markets. Office 365 revenue overtook traditional license sales for Office in 2017.

Editions

Microsoft Office is available in several editions, which regroup a given number of applications for a specific price. Primarily, Microsoft sells Office as Microsoft 365. The editions are as follows:

- Microsoft 365 Personal
- Microsoft 365 Family
- Microsoft 365 Business Basic
- Microsoft 365 Business Standard
- Microsoft 365 Business Premium
- Microsoft 365 apps for business
- Microsoft 365 apps for enterprise
- Office 365 E1, E3, E5
- Office 365 A1, A3, A5 (for education)
- Office 365 G1, G3, G5 (for government)
- Microsoft 365 F1, F3, Office 365 F3 (for frontline)

Microsoft sells Office for a one-time purchase as Home & Student and Home & Business, however, these editions do not receive major updates.

Education pricing

Post-secondary students may obtain the university edition of Microsoft Office 365 subscription. It is limited to one user and two devices, plus the subscription price is valid for four years instead of just one. Apart from this, the university edition is identical in features to the Home Premium version. This marks the first time Microsoft does not offer physical or permanent software at academic pricing, in contrast to the university versions of Office 2010 and Office 2011. In addition, students eligible for DreamSpark program may receive select standalone Microsoft Office apps free of charge.

Discontinued applications and features

- Binder was an application that can incorporate several documents into one file and was originally designed as a container system for storing related documents in a single file. The complexity of use and learning curve led to little usage, and it was discontinued after Office XP.
- Bookshelf was a reference collection introduced in 1987 as part of Microsoft's extensive work in promoting CD-ROM technology as a distribution medium for electronic publishing.
- Data Analyzer was a business intelligence program for graphical visualization of data and its analysis.
- Docs.com was a public document sharing service where Office users can upload and share Word, Excel, PowerPoint, Sway and PDF files for the whole world to discover and use.
- Entourage was an Outlook counterpart on macOS, Microsoft discontinued it in favor of extending the Outlook brand name.
- FrontPage was a WYSIWYG HTML editor and website administration tool for Windows. It was branded as part of the Microsoft Office suite from 1997 to 2003. FrontPage was discontinued in December 2006 and replaced by Microsoft SharePoint Designer and Microsoft Expression Web.
- InfoPath was a Windows application for designing and distributing rich XML-based forms. The last version was included in Office 2013.[70]
- InterConnect was a business-relationship database available only in Japan.
- Internet Explorer was a graphical web browser and one of the main participants of the first browser war. It was included in Office until Office XP when it was removed.
- Mail was a mail client (in old versions of Office, later replaced by Microsoft Schedule Plus and subsequently Microsoft Outlook).
- Office Accounting (formerly Small Business Accounting) was an accounting software application from Microsoft targeted towards small businesses that had between 1 and 25 employees.
- Office Assistant (included since Office 97 on Windows and Office 98 on Mac as a part of Microsoft Agent technology) was a system that uses animated characters to offer context-sensitive suggestions to users and access to the help system. The

Assistant is often dubbed "Clippy" or "Clippit", due to its default to a paper clip character, coded as CLIPPIT.ACS. The latest versions that include the Office Assistant were Office 2003 (Windows) and Office 2004 (Mac).

- Office Document Image Writer was a virtual printer that takes documents from Microsoft Office or any other application and prints them, or stores them in an image file as TIFF or Microsoft Document Imaging Format format. It was discontinued with Office 2010.[71]
- Office Document Imaging was an application that supports editing scanned documents. Discontinued Office 2010.[71]
- Office Document Scanning was a scanning and OCR application. Discontinued Office 2010.[71]
- Office Picture Manager was a basic photo management software (similar to Google's Picasa or Adobe's Photoshop Elements), that replaced Microsoft Photo Editor.
- PhotoDraw was a graphics program that was first released as part of the Office 2000 Premium Edition. A later version for Windows XP compatibility was released, known as PhotoDraw 2000 Version 2. Microsoft discontinued the program in 2001.
- Photo Editor was photo-editing or raster-graphics software in older Office versions up to Office XP. It was supplemented by Microsoft PhotoDraw in Office 2000 Premium edition.
- Schedule Plus (also shown as Schedule+) was released with Office 95. It featured a planner, to-do list, and contact information. Its functions were incorporated into Microsoft Outlook.
- SharePoint Designer was a WYSIWYG HTML editor and website administration tool. Microsoft attempted to turn it into a specialized HTML editor for SharePoint sites, but failed on this project and wanted to discontinue it.
- SharePoint Workspace (formerly Groove) was a proprietary peer-to-peer document collaboration software designed for teams with members who are regularly offline or who do not share the same network security clearance.
- Skype for Business was an integrated communications client for conferences and meetings in real-time; it is the only Microsoft Office desktop app that is neither

useful without a proper network infrastructure nor has the "Microsoft" prefix in its name.

- Streets & Trips (known in other countries as Microsoft AutoRoute) is a discontinued mapping program developed and distributed by Microsoft.
- Unbind is a program that can extract the contents of a Binder file. Unbind can be installed from the Office XP CD-ROM.
- Virtual PC was included with Microsoft Office Professional Edition 2004 for Mac. Microsoft discontinued support for Virtual PC on the Mac in 2006 owing to new Macs possessing the same Intel architecture as Windows PCs.[72] It emulated a standard PC and its hardware.
- Vizact was a program that "activated" documents using HTML, adding effects such as animation. It allows users to create dynamic documents for the Web. The development has ended due to unpopularity.

Discontinued server applications

- Microsoft Office Forms Server lets users use any browser to access and fill InfoPath forms. Office Forms Server is a standalone server installation of InfoPath Forms Services.
- Microsoft Office Groove Server was centrally managing all deployments of Microsoft Office Groove in the enterprise.
- Microsoft Office Project Portfolio Server allows creation of a project portfolio, including workflows, which is hosted centrally.
- Microsoft Office PerformancePoint Server allows customers to monitor, analyze, and plan their business.

Discontinued web services

- Office Live

- Office Live Small Business had web hosting services and online collaboration tools for small businesses.
- Office Live Workspace had online storage and collaboration service for documents, which was superseded by Office on the web.

- Office Live Meeting was a web conferencing service.

Criticism

Data formats

Microsoft Office has been criticized in the past for using proprietary file formats rather than open standards, which forces users who share data into adopting the same software platform. However, on February 15, 2008, Microsoft made the entire documentation for the binary Office formats freely available under the Open Specification Promise. Also, Office Open XML, the document format for the latest versions of Office for Windows and Mac, has been standardized under both Ecma International and ISO. Ecma International has published the Office Open XML specification free of copyrights and Microsoft has granted patent rights to the formats technology under the Open Specification Promise and has made available free downloadable converters for previous versions of Microsoft Office including Office 2003, Office XP, Office 2000 and Office 2004 for the Mac. Third-party implementations of Office Open XML exist on the Mac platform (iWork 08) and Linux (OpenOffice.org 2.3 – Novell Edition only).

Unicode and bi-directional texts

Another point of criticism Microsoft Office has faced was the lack of support in its Mac versions for Unicode and Bi-directional text languages, notably Arabic and Hebrew. This issue, which had existed since the first release in 1989, was addressed in the 2016 version.

Privacy

On November 13, 2018, a report initiated by the Government of the Netherlands concluded that Microsoft Office 2016 and Office 365 do not comply with GDPR, the European law which regulates data protection and privacy for all citizens in and outside the EU and EFTA region. The investigation was initiated by the observation that Microsoft does not reveal or share publicly any data collected about users of its software. In addition, the company does not provide users of its (Office) software an option to turn off diagnostic and telemetry data sent back to the company. Researchers found that most of the data that the Microsoft software collects and "sends home" is diagnostics. Researchers also observed that Microsoft "seemingly tried to make the system GDPR compliant by storing Office documents on servers based in the EU". However, they discovered the software packages collected additional data that contained private user information, some of which was stored on servers located in the US. The Netherlands Ministry of Justice hired Privacy Company to probe and evaluate the use of Microsoft Office products in the public sector. "Microsoft systematically collects data on a large scale about the individual use of Word, Excel, PowerPoint, and Outlook. Covertly, without informing people", researchers of the Privacy Company stated in their blog post. "Microsoft does not offer any choice with regard to the amount of data, or possibility to switch off the collection, or ability to see what data are collected, because the data stream is encoded."

The researchers commented that there is no need for Microsoft to store information such as IPs and email addresses, which are collected automatically by the software. "Microsoft should not store these transient, functional data, unless the retention is strictly necessary, for example, for security purposes", the researchers conclude in the final report by the Netherlands Ministry of Justice.

As a result of this in-depth study and its conclusions, the Netherlands regulatory body concluded that Microsoft has violated GDPR "on many counts" including "lack of transparency and purpose limitation, and the lack of a legal ground for the processing." Microsoft has provided the Dutch authorities with an "improvement plan" that should satisfy Dutch regulators that it "would end all violations". The Dutch regulatory body is monitoring the situation and states that "If progress is deemed insufficient or if the improvements offered are unsatisfactory, SLM Microsoft Rijk will reconsider its position and may ask the Dutch Data Protection Authority to carry out a prior consultation and to impose enforcement measures." When asked for a response by an IT professional publication, a Microsoft spokesperson stated: "We are committed to our customers' privacy, putting them in control of their data and ensuring that Office ProPlus and other Microsoft products and services comply with GDPR and other applicable laws. We appreciate the opportunity to discuss our diagnostic data handling practices in Office ProPlus with the Dutch Ministry of Justice and look forward to a successful resolution of any concerns." The user privacy data issue affects

ProPlus subscriptions of Microsoft Office 2016 and Microsoft Office 365, including the online version of Microsoft Office 365.

Microsoft Office 4.x

Microsoft Office 4.0 was released containing Word 6.0, Excel 4.0a, PowerPoint 3.0 and Mail in 1993. Word's version number jumped from 2.0 to 6.0 so that it would have the same version number as the MS-DOS and Macintosh versions (Excel and PowerPoint were already numbered the same as the Macintosh versions).

Microsoft Office 4.2 for Windows NT was released in 1994 for i386, Alpha, MIPS and PowerPC architectures, containing Word 6.0 and Excel 5.0 (both 32-bit, PowerPoint 4.0 (16-bit), and Microsoft Office Manager 4.2 (the precursor to the Office Shortcut Bar)).

Microsoft Office 95

Microsoft Office 95 was released on August 24, 1995. Software version numbers were altered again to create parity across the suite – every program was called version 7.0 meaning all but Word missed out versions. Office 95 included new components to the suite such as Schedule+ and Binder.

Office for Windows 95 was designed as a fully 32-bit version to match Windows 95 although some apps not bundled as part of the suite at that time - Publisher for Windows 95 and Project 95 had some 16-bit components even though their main program executable was 32-bit.

Office 95 was available in two versions, Office 95 Standard and Office 95 Professional. The standard version consisted of Word 7.0, Excel 7.0, PowerPoint 7.0, and Schedule+ 7.0. The professional edition contained all of the items in the standard version plus Access 7.0. If the professional version was purchased in CD-ROM form, it also included Bookshelf.

The logo used in Office 95 returns in Office 97, 2000 and XP. Microsoft Office 98 Macintosh Edition also uses a similar logo.

Microsoft Office 97

Microsoft Office 97 (Office 8.0) included hundreds of new features and improvements, such as introducing command bars, a paradigm in which menus and toolbars were made more similar in capability and visual design. Office 97 also featured Natural Language Systems and grammar checking. Office 97 featured new components to the suite including FrontPage 97, Expedia Streets 98 (in Small Business Edition), and Internet Explorer 3.0 & 4.0.

Office 97 was the first version of Office to include the Office Assistant. In Brazil, it was also the first version to introduce the Registration Wizard, a precursor to Microsoft Product Activation. With this release, the accompanying apps, Project 98 and Publisher 98 also transitioned to fully 32-bit versions. Exchange Server, a mail server and calendaring server developed by Microsoft, is the server for Outlook after discontinuing Exchange Client.

Microsoft Office 2000

Microsoft Office 2000 (Office 9.0) introduced adaptive menus, where little-used options were hidden from the user. It also introduced a new security feature, built around digital signatures, to diminish the threat of macro viruses.

The Microsoft Script Editor, an optional tool that can edit script code, was also introduced in Office 2000. Office 2000 automatically trusts macros (written in VBA 6) that were digitally signed from authors who have been previously designated as trusted. Office 2000 also introduces PhotoDraw, a raster and vector imaging program, as well as Web Components, Visio, and Vizact.

The Registration Wizard, a precursor to Microsoft Product Activation, remained in Brazil and was also extended to Australia and New Zealand, though not for volume-licensed editions. Academic software in the United States and Canada also featured the Registration Wizard.

Microsoft Office XP

Microsoft Office XP (Office 10.0 or Office 2002) was released in conjunction with Windows XP, and was a major upgrade with numerous enhancements and changes over Office 2000. Office XP introduced the Safe Mode feature, which allows applications such as Outlook to boot when it might otherwise fail by bypassing a corrupted registry or a faulty add-in. Smart tag is a technology introduced with Office XP in Word and Excel and discontinued in Office 2010.

Office XP also introduces new components including Document Imaging, Document Scanning, Clip Organizer, MapPoint, and Data Analyzer. Binder was replaced by Unbind, a program that can extract the contents of a Binder file. Unbind can be installed from the Office XP CD-ROM.

Office XP includes integrated voice command and text dictation capabilities, as well as handwriting recognition. It was the first version to require Microsoft Product Activation worldwide and in all editions as an anti-piracy measure, which attracted widespread controversy. Product Activation remained absent from Office for Mac releases until it was introduced in Office 2011 for Mac.

Microsoft Office 2003

Microsoft Office 2003 (Office 11.0) was released in 2003. It featured a new logo. Two new applications made their debut in Office 2003: Microsoft InfoPath and OneNote. It is the first version to use new, more colorful icons. Outlook 2003 provides improved functionality in many areas, including Kerberos authentication, RPC over HTTP, Cached Exchange Mode, and an improved junk mail filter.

Office 2003 introduces three new programs to the Office product lineup: InfoPath, a program for designing, filling, and submitting electronic structured data forms; OneNote, a note-taking program for creating and organizing diagrams, graphics, handwritten notes, recorded audio, and text; and the Picture Manager graphics software which can open, manage, and share digital images.

SharePoint, a web collaboration platform codenamed as Office Server, has integration and compatibility with Office 2003 and so on.

Microsoft Office 2007

Microsoft Office 2007 (Office 12.0) was released in 2007. Office 2007's new features include a new graphical user interface called the Fluent User Interface, replacing the menus and toolbars that have been the cornerstone of Office since its inception with a tabbed toolbar, known as the Ribbon; new XML-based file formats called Office Open XML; and the inclusion of Groove, a collaborative software application.

While Microsoft removed Data Analyzer, FrontPage, Vizact, and Schedule+ from Office 2007; they also added Communicator, Groove, SharePoint Designer, and Office Customization Tool (OCT) to the suite.

Microsoft Office 2010

Microsoft Office 2010 (Office 14.0, Microsoft skipped 13.0 due to fear of 13) was finalized on April 15, 2010, and made available to consumers on June 15, 2010. The main features of Office 2010 include the backstage file menu, new collaboration tools, a customizable ribbon, protected view and a navigation panel. Office Communicator, an instant messaging and videotelephony application, was renamed into Lync 2010.

This is the first version to ship in 32-bit and 64-bit variants. Microsoft Office 2010 featured a new logo, which resembled the 2007 logo, except in gold, and with a modification in shape. Microsoft released Service Pack 1 for Office 2010 on June 28, 2011 and Service Pack 2 on July 16, 2013. Office Online was first released online along with SkyDrive, an online storing service.

Microsoft Office 2013

A technical preview of Microsoft Office 2013 (Build 15.0.3612.1010) was released on January 30, 2012, and a Customer Preview version was made available to consumers on July 16, 2012. It sports a revamped application interface; the interface is based on Metro, the interface of Windows Phone and Windows 8. Microsoft Outlook has received the most pronounced changes so far; for example, the Metro interface provides a new visualization for scheduled tasks. PowerPoint includes more templates and transition effects, and OneNote includes a new splash screen.

On May 16, 2011, new images of Office 15 were revealed, showing Excel with a tool for filtering data in a timeline, the ability to convert Roman numerals to Arabic numerals, and the integration of advanced trigonometric functions. In Word, the capability of inserting video and audio online as well as the broadcasting of documents on the Web were implemented. Microsoft has promised support for Office Open XML Strict starting with version 15, a format Microsoft has submitted to the ISO for interoperability with other office suites, and to aid adoption in the public sector. This version can read and write ODF 1.2 (Windows only).

On October 24, 2012, Office 2013 Professional Plus was released to manufacturing and was made available to TechNet and MSDN subscribers for download. On November 15, 2012, the 60-day trial version was released for public download. Office 2013 was released to general availability on January 29, 2013. Service Pack 1 for Office 2013 was released on February 25, 2014. Some applications were completely removed from the entire suite including SharePoint Workspace, Clip Organizer, and Office Picture Manager.

Microsoft Office 2016

On January 22, 2015, the Microsoft Office blog announced that the next version of the suite for Windows desktop, Office 2016, was in development. On May 4, 2015, a public preview of Microsoft Office 2016 was released. Office 2016 was released for Mac OS X on July 9, 2015 and for Windows on September 22, 2015.

Users who had the Professional Plus 2016 subscription have the new Skype for Business app. Microsoft Teams, a team collaboration program meant to rival Slack, was released as a separate product for business and enterprise users.

Microsoft Office 2019

On September 26, 2017, Microsoft announced that the next version of the suite for Windows desktop, Office 2019, was in development. On April 27, 2018, Microsoft released Office 2019 Commercial Preview for Windows 10. It was released to general availability for Windows 10 and for macOS on September 24, 2018.

Microsoft Office 2021

On February 18, 2021, Microsoft announced that the next version of the suite for Windows desktop, Office 2021, was in development. This new version will be supported for five years and was released on October 5, 2021.

Mac versions

Prior to packaging its various office-type Mac OS software applications into Office, Microsoft released Mac versions of Word 1.0 in 1984, the first year of the Macintosh computer; Excel 1.0 in 1985; and PowerPoint 1.0 in 1987. Microsoft does not include its Access database application in Office for Mac.

Microsoft has noted that some features are added to Office for Mac before they appear in Windows versions, such as Office for Mac 2001's Office Project Gallery and PowerPoint Movie feature, which allows users to save presentations as QuickTime movies. However, Microsoft Office for Mac has been long criticized for its lack of support of Unicode and for its lack of support for right-to-left languages, notably Arabic, Hebrew and Persian.

Early Office for Mac releases (1989–1994)

Microsoft Office for Mac was introduced for Mac OS in 1989, before Office was released for Windows. It included Word 4.0, Excel 2.2, PowerPoint 2.01, and Mail 1.37. It was originally a limited-time promotion but later became a regular product. With the release of Office on CD-ROM later that year, Microsoft became the first major Mac publisher to put its applications on CD-ROM.

Microsoft Office 1.5 for Mac was released in 1991 and included the updated Excel 3.0, the first application to support Apple's System 7 operating system. Microsoft Office 3.0 for Mac was released in 1992 and included Word 5.0, Excel 4.0, PowerPoint 3.0 and Mail Client. Excel 4.0 was the first application to support new AppleScript.

Microsoft Office 4.2 for Mac was released in 1994. (Version 4.0 was skipped to synchronize version numbers with Office for Windows) Version 4.2 included Word 6.0, Excel 5.0, PowerPoint 4.0 and Mail 3.2. It was the first Office suite for Power Macintosh. Its user interface was identical to Office 4.2 for Windows leading many customers to comment that it wasn't Mac-like enough. The final release for Mac 68K was Office 4.2.1, which updated Word to version 6.0.1, somewhat improving performance.

Microsoft Officc 98 Macintosh Edition

Microsoft Office 98 Macintosh Edition was unveiled at MacWorld Expo/San Francisco in 1998. It introduced the Internet Explorer 4.0 web browser and Outlook Express, an Internet e-mail client and usenet newsgroup reader. Office 98 was re-engineered by Microsoft's Macintosh Business Unit to satisfy customers' desire for software they felt was more Mac-like. It included drag–and-drop installation, self-repairing applications and Quick Thesaurus, before such features were available in Office for Windows. It also was the first version to support QuickTime movies.

Microsoft Office 2001 and v. X

Microsoft Office 2001 was launched in 2000 as the last Office suite for the classic Mac OS. It required a PowerPC processor. This version introduced Entourage, an e-mail client that included information management tools such as a calendar, an address book, task lists and notes. Microsoft Office v. X was released in 2001 and was the first version of Microsoft Office for Mac OS X. Support for Office v. X ended on January 9, 2007, after the release of the final update, 10.1.9 Office v.X includes Word X, Excel X, PowerPoint X, Entourage X, MSN Messenger for Mac and Windows Media Player 9 for Mac; it was the last version of Office for Mac to include Internet Explorer for Mac.

Office 2004

Microsoft Office 2004 for Mac was released on May 11, 2004. It includes Microsoft Word, Excel, PowerPoint, Entourage and Virtual PC. It is the final version of Office to be built exclusively for PowerPC and to officially support G3 processors, as its sequel lists a G4, G5, or Intel processor as a requirement. It was notable for supporting Visual Basic for Applications (VBA), which is unavailable in Office 2008. This led Microsoft to extend support for Office 2004 from October 13, 2009, to January 10, 2012. VBA functionality was reintroduced in Office 2011, which is only compatible with Intel processors.

Office 2008

Microsoft Office 2008 for Mac was released on January 15, 2008. It was the only Office for Mac suite to be compiled as a universal binary, being the first to feature native Intel support and the last to feature PowerPC support for G4 and G5 processors, although the suite is unofficially compatible with G3 processors. New features include native Office Open XML file format support, which debuted in Office 2007 for Windows, and stronger Microsoft Office password protection employing AES-128 and SHA-1. Benchmarks suggested that compared to its predecessor, Office 2008 ran at similar speeds on Intel machines and slower speeds on PowerPC machines. Office 2008 also lacked Visual Basic for Applications (VBA) support, leaving it with only 15 months of additional mainstream support compared to its predecessor. Nevertheless, five months after it was released, Microsoft said that Office 2008 was "selling faster than any previous version of Office for Mac in the past 19 years" and affirmed "its commitment to future products for the Mac."

Office 2011

Microsoft Office for Mac 2011 was released on October 26, 2010,. It is the first version of Office for Mac to be compiled exclusively for Intel processors, dropping support for the PowerPC architecture. It features an OS X version of Outlook to replace the Entourage email client. This version of Outlook is intended to make the OS X version of Office work better with Microsoft's Exchange server and with those using

Office for Windows. Office 2011 includes a Mac-based Ribbon similar to Office for Windows.

OneNote and Outlook release (2014)

Microsoft OneNote for Mac was released on March 17, 2014. It marks the company's first release of the note-taking software on the Mac. It is available as a free download to all users of the Mac App Store in OS X Mavericks.

Microsoft Outlook 2016 for Mac debuted on October 31, 2014. It requires a paid Office 365 subscription, meaning that traditional Office 2011 retail or volume licenses cannot activate this version of Outlook. On that day, Microsoft confirmed that it would release the next version of Office for Mac in late 2015.

Despite dropping support for older versions of OS X and only keeping support for 64-bit-only versions of OS X, these versions of OneNote and Outlook are 32-bit applications like their predecessors.

Office 2016

The first Preview version of Microsoft Office 2016 for Mac was released on March 5, 2015. On July 9, 2015, Microsoft released the final version of Microsoft Office 2016 for Mac which includes Word, Excel, PowerPoint, Outlook and OneNote. It was immediately made available for Office 365 subscribers with either a Home, Personal, Business, Business Premium, E3 or ProPlus subscription. A non–Office 365 edition of Office 2016 was made available as a one-time purchase option on September 22, 2015.

Office 2019

Mobile versions

Office Mobile for iPhone was released on June 14, 2013, in the United States. Support for 135 markets and 27 languages was rolled out over a few days. It requires iOS 8 or later. Although the app also works on iPad devices, excluding the first generation, it is designed for a small screen. Office Mobile was released for Android phones on July 31, 2013, in the United States. Support for 117 markets and 33 languages was added gradually over several weeks. It is supported on Android 4.0 and later. Office Mobile is or was also available, though no longer supported, on Windows Mobile, Windows Phone and Symbian. Windows RT devices (such as Microsoft Surface) were bundled with "Office RT", a port of the PC version of Office 2013 to ARM architecture. The applications contain most of the functionality available in their versions for Intel-compatible PCs, but some features have been removed.

Early Office Mobile releases

Originally called Office Mobile which was shipped initially as "Pocket Office", was released by Microsoft with the Windows CE 1.0 operating system in 1996. This release was specifically for the Handheld PC hardware platform, as Windows Mobile Smartphone and Pocket PC hardware specifications had not yet been released. It consisted of Pocket Word and Pocket Excel; PowerPoint, Access, and Outlook were added later. With steady updates throughout subsequent releases of Windows Mobile, Office Mobile was rebranded as its current name after the release of the Windows Mobile 5.0 operating system. This release of Office Mobile also included PowerPoint Mobile for the first time. Accompanying the release of Microsoft OneNote 2007, a new optional addition to the Office Mobile line of programs was released as OneNote Mobile. With the release of Windows Mobile 6 Standard, Office Mobile became available for the Smartphone hardware platform, but unlike Office Mobile for the Professional and Classic versions of Windows Mobile, creation of new documents is not an added feature. A popular workaround is to create a new blank document in a desktop version of Office, synchronize it to the device, and then edit and save on the Windows Mobile device.

In June 2007, Microsoft announced a new version of the office suite, Office Mobile 2007. It became available as "Office Mobile 6.1" on September 26, 2007, as a free upgrade download to current Windows Mobile 5.0 and 6 users. However, "Office Mobile 6.1 Upgrade" is not compatible with Windows Mobile 5.0 powered devices running builds earlier than 14847. It is a pre-installed feature in subsequent releases of Windows Mobile 6 devices. Office Mobile 6.1 is compatible with the Office Open XML specification like its desktop counterpart.

On August 12, 2009, it was announced that Office Mobile would also be released for the Symbian platform as a joint agreement between Microsoft and Nokia. It was the first time Microsoft would develop Office mobile applications for another smartphone platform. The first application to appear on Nokia Eseries smartphones was Microsoft Office Communicator. In February 2012, Microsoft released OneNote, Lync 2010, Document Connection and PowerPoint Broadcast for Symbian. In April, Word Mobile, PowerPoint Mobile and Excel Mobile joined the Office Suite.

On October 21, 2010, Microsoft debuted Office Mobile 2010 with the release of Windows Phone 7. In Windows Phone, users can access and edit documents directly off of their SkyDrive or Office 365 accounts in a dedicated Office hub. The Office Hub, which is preinstalled into the operating system, contains Word, PowerPoint and Excel. The operating system also includes OneNote, although not as a part of the Office Hub. Lync is not included, but can be downloaded as standalone app from the Windows Phone Store free of charge.

In October 2012, Microsoft released a new version of Microsoft Office Mobile for Windows Phone 8 and Windows Phone 7.8.

Office for Android, iOS and Windows 10 Mobile

Office Mobile was released for iPhone on June 14, 2013, and for Android phones on July 31, 2013. In March 2014, Microsoft released Office Lens, a scanner app that enhances photos. Photos are then attached to an Office document. Office Lens is an app in the Windows Phone store, as well as built into the camera functionality in the OneNote apps for iOS and Windows 8.

On March 27, 2014, Microsoft launched Office for iPad, the first dedicated version of Office for tablet computers. In addition, Microsoft made the Android and iOS versions of Office Mobile free for 'home use' on phones, although the company still requires an Office 365 subscription for using Office Mobile for business use. On November 6, 2014, Office was subsequently made free for personal use on the iPad in addition to phones. As part of this announcement, Microsoft also split up its single "Office suite" app on iPhones into separate, standalone apps for Word, Excel and PowerPoint, released a revamped version of Office Mobile for iPhone, added direct integration with Dropbox, and previewed future versions of Office for other platforms.

Office for Android tablets was released on January 29, 2015, following a successful two-month preview period. These apps allow users to edit and create documents for free on devices with screen sizes of 10.1 inches or less, though as with the iPad versions, an Office 365 subscription is required to unlock premium features and for commercial use of the apps. Tablets with screen sizes larger than 10.1 inches are also supported, but, as was originally the case with the iPad version, are restricted to viewing documents only unless a valid Office 365 subscription is used to enable editing and document creation.

On January 21, 2015, during the "Windows 10: The Next Chapter" press event, Microsoft unveiled Office for Windows 10, Windows Runtime ports of the Android and iOS versions of the Office Mobile suite. Optimized for smartphones and tablets, they are universal apps that can run on both Windows and Windows for phones, and share similar underlying code. A simplified version of Outlook was also added to the suite. They will be bundled with Windows 10 mobile devices, and available from the Windows Store for the PC version of Windows 10. Although the preview versions were free for most editing, the release versions will require an Office 365 subscription on larger tablets (screen size larger than 10.1 inches) and desktops for editing, as with large Android tablets. Smaller tablets and phones will have most editing features for free.

On June 24, 2015, Microsoft released Word, Excel and PowerPoint as standalone apps on Google Play for Android phones, following a one-month preview. These apps have also been bundled with Android devices from major OEMs, as a result of

Microsoft tying distribution of them and Skype to patent-licensing agreements related to the Android platform. The Android version is also supported on certain ChromeOS machines.

On February 19, 2020, Microsoft announced a new unified Office mobile app for Android and iOS. This app combines Word, Excel, and PowerPoint into a single app and introduces new capabilities as making quick notes, signing PDFs, scanning QR codes, and transferring files.

Online versions

Office Web Apps was first revealed in October 2008 at PDC 2008 in Los Angeles. Chris Capossela, senior vice president of Microsoft business division, introduced Office Web Apps as lightweight versions of Word, Excel, PowerPoint and OneNote that allow people to create, edit and collaborate on Office documents through a web browser. According to Capossela, Office Web Apps was to become available as a part of Office Live Workspace. Office Web Apps was announced to be powered by AJAX as well as Silverlight; however, the latter is optional and its availability will only "enhance the user experience, resulting in sharper images and improved rendering." Microsoft's Business Division President Stephen Elop stated during PDC 2008 that "a technology preview of Office Web Apps would become available later in 2008". However, the Technical Preview of Office Web Apps was not released until 2009.

On July 13, 2009, Microsoft announced at its Worldwide Partners Conference 2009 in New Orleans that Microsoft Office 2010 reached its "Technical Preview" development milestone and features of Office Web Apps were demonstrated to the public for the first time. Additionally, Microsoft announced that Office Web Apps would be made available to consumers online and free of charge, while Microsoft Software Assurance customers will have the option of running them on premises. Office 2010 beta testers were not given access to Office Web Apps at this date, and it was announced that it would be available for testers during August 2009. However, in August 2009, a Microsoft spokesperson stated that there had been a delay in the release of Office Web Apps Technical Preview and it would not be available by the end of August.

Microsoft officially released the Technical Preview of Office Web Apps on September 17, 2009. Office Web Apps was made available to selected testers via its OneDrive (at the time Skydrive) service. The final version of Office Web Apps was made available to the public via Windows Live Office on June 7, 2010.

On October 22, 2012, Microsoft announced the release of new features including co-authoring, performance improvements and touch support.

On November 6, 2013, Microsoft announced further new features including real-time co-authoring and an Auto-Save feature in Word (replacing the save button).

In February 2014, Office Web Apps were re-branded Office Online and incorporated into other Microsoft web services, including Calendar, OneDrive, Outlook.com, and People. Microsoft had previously attempted to unify its online services suite (including Microsoft Passport, Hotmail, MSN Messenger, and later SkyDrive) under a brand known as Windows Live, first launched in 2005. However, with the impending launch of Windows 8 and its increased use of cloud services, Microsoft dropped the Windows Live brand to emphasize that these services would now be built directly into Windows and not merely be a "bolted on" add-on. Critics had criticized the Windows Live brand for having no clear vision, as it was being applied to an increasingly broad array of unrelated services. At the same time, Windows Live Hotmail was relaunched as Outlook.com (sharing its name with the Microsoft Outlook personal information manager).

In July 2019, Microsoft announced that they were retiring the "Online" branding for Office Online. The product is now Office, and may be referred to as "Office for the web" or "Office in a browser".

MS OFFICE

Microsoft Office is a suite of productivity applications developed by Microsoft Corporation. It includes programs such as Word, Excel, PowerPoint, Outlook, Access, Publisher, and OneNote. Each program is designed to help users create, manage, and share various types of documents, spreadsheets, presentations, emails, and other digital content.

Microsoft Office is available for both Windows and Mac operating systems, and it is widely used in both personal and professional settings. It offers many features and tools to enhance productivity, such as templates, collaboration options, formatting tools, and automation capabilities.

Microsoft Office is available as a subscription-based service called Microsoft 365, which provides regular updates and access to the latest features. It can also be purchased as a one-time license for a specific version, such as Office 2019.

Microsoft Office is a software which was developed by Microsoft in 1988. This Office suite comprises various applications which form the core of computer usage in today's world.

From the examination point of view, questions from MS Office and its applications are frequently asked in all the major Government Exams conducted in the country.

In this article, we shall discuss at length Microsoft Office, its applications, important notes to prepare for the upcoming examinations and some sample questions and answers for the reference of candidates.

Competitive exams including Bank, SSC, Railways, Insurance, etc. have Computer Knowledge as an integral part of their exam syllabus and candidates must note that it can be the most scoring too.

No lengthy calculations or solutions are required to answer Computer knowledge-based questions and instead of complex questions, straightforward and direct questions are asked which makes answering them even easier.

Introduction

Microsoft Office (or simply Office) is a family of server software, and services developed by Microsoft. It was first announced by Bill Gates on August 1, 1988, in Las Vegas. The first version of Office contained Microsoft Word, Microsoft Excel, and Microsoft PowerPoint. Over the years, Office applications have grown substantially closer with shared features such as a common spell checker, data integration etc. Office is produced in several versions targeted towards different end-users and computing environments. The original, and most widely used version, is the desktop version, available for PCs running the Windows, Linux and Mac OS operating systems. Office Online is a version of the software that runs within a web browser, while Microsoft also maintains Office apps for Android and iOS.

Microsoft Office is a suite of desktop productivity applications that is designed specifically to be used for office or business use. It is a proprietary product of Microsoft Corporation and was first released in 1990. Microsoft Office is available in 35 different languages and is supported by Windows, Mac and most Linux variants. It mainly consists of Word, Excel, PowerPoint, Access, OneNote, Outlook and Publisher applications.

Microsoft Office was primarily created to automate the manual office work with a collection of purpose-built applications.

Each of the applications in Microsoft Office serves as specific knowledge or office domain such as:

1. Microsoft Word: Helps users in creating text documents.
2. Microsoft Excel: Creates simple to complex data/numerical spreadsheets.
3. Microsoft PowerPoint: Stand-alone application for creating professional multimedia presentations.
4. Microsoft Access: Database management application.
5. Microsoft Publisher: Introductory application for creating and publishing marketing materials.

6. Microsoft OneNote: Alternate to a paper notebook, it enables an user to neatly organize their notes.

MS Office Applications & its Functions

Currently, MS Office 2016 version is being used across the world and all its applications are widely used for personal and professional purposes.

Discussed below are the applications of Microsoft Office along with each of their functions.

1. MS Word

First released on October 25, 1983 Extension for Doc files is ".doc" It is useful in creating text documents Templates can be created for Professional use with the help of MS Word Work Art, colours, images, animations can be added along with the text in the same file which is downloadable in the form of a document Authors can use for writing/ editing their work To read in detail about Microsoft Word, its features, uses and to get some sample questions based on this program of Office suite, visit the linked article.

2. MS Excel

Majorly used for making spreadsheets A spreadsheet consists of grids in the form of rows and columns which is easy to manage and can be used as a replacement for paper It is a data processing application Large data can easily be managed and saved in tabular format using MS Excel Calculations can be done based on the large amount of data entered into the cells of a spreadsheet within seconds File extension, when saved in the computer, is ".xls" Also, visit the Microsoft Excel page to get more information regarding this spreadsheet software and its components.

3. MS PowerPoint

It was released on April 20, 1987 Used to create audiovisual presentations Each presentation is made up of various slides displaying data/ information Each slide may contain audio, video, graphics, text, bullet numbering, tables etc. The extension for PowerPoint presentations is ".ppt" Used majorly for professional usage Using

PowerPoint, presentations can be made more interactive In terms of Graphical user interface, using MS PowerPoint, interesting and appealing presentation and documents can be created. To read more about its features and usage, candidates can visit the linked article.

4. MS Access

It was released on November 13, 1992 It is Database Management Software (DBMS) Table, queries, forms and reports can be created on MS Access Import and export of data into other formats can be done The file extension is ".accdb"

5. MS Outlook

It was released on January 16, 1997 It is a personal information management system It can be used both as a single-user application or multi-user software Its functions also include task managing, calendaring, contact managing, journal logging and web browsing It is the email client of the Office Suite The file extension for an Outlook file is ".pst"

6. MS OneNote

It was released on November 19, 2003 It is a note-taking application When introduced, it was a part of the Office suite only. Later, the developers made it free, standalone and easily available at play store for android devices The notes may include images, text, tables, etc. The extension for OneNote files is ".one" It can be used both online and offline and is a multi-user application.

Important Features of Ms-Word

Ms-Word not only supports word processing features but also DTP features. Some of the important features of Ms-Word are listed below:

1. Using word you can create the document and edit them later, as and when required, by adding more text, modifying the existing text, deleting/moving some part of it.
2. Changing the size of the margins can reformat complete document or part of text.
3. Font size and type of fonts can also be changed. Page numbers and Header and Footer can be included.

4. Spelling can be checked and correction can be made automatically in the entire document. Word count and other statistics can be generated.
5. Text can be formatted in columnar style as we see in the newspaper. Text boxes can be made.
6. Tables can be made and included in the text.
7. Word also allows the user to mix the graphical pictures with the text. Graphical pictures can either be created in word itself or can be imported from outside like from Clip Art Gallery.
8. Word also has the facility of macros. Macros can be either attached to some function/special keys or to a tool bar or to a menu.
9. It also provides online help of any option.

Introduction to Ms-Power Point

A PowerPoint presentation is a presentation created using Microsoft PowerPoint software. The presentation is a collection of individual slides that contain information on a topic. PowerPoint presentations are commonly used in business meetings and for training and educational purposes. Microsoft PowerPoint is a software product used to perform computerbased presentations. There are various circumstances in which a presentation is made: teaching a class, introducing a product to sell, explaining an organizational structure, etc. The preparation and the actual delivery of each are quite different. PowerPoint typically comes with a set of preloaded themes for you to choose from. These can range from simple color changes to complete format layouts with accompanying font text. Themes can be applied through the whole presentation or a single slide. Using the page setup allows you to optimize the presentation for the display size; for instance, you should use a larger screen ratio when displaying on a projector compared to a computer screen.

Features

PowerPoint software features and formatting options include a wizard that walks you through the presentation creation process. Design templates---prepackaged background designs and font styles that will be applied to all slides in a presentation. When viewing a presentation, slide progression can be manual, using the computer mouse or keyboard to progress to the next slide, or slides can be set up to progress after a specified length of time. Slide introductions and transitions can be added to the slides.

Introduction to Ms-Excel

Microsoft Excel is a general-purpose electronic spreadsheet used to organize, calculate, and analyze data. The task you can complete with Excel ranges from preparing a simple family budget, preparing a purchase order, or managing a complex accounting ledger for a medium size business.

Excel Features

There are a number of features that are available in Excel to make your task easier. Some of the main features are:

AutoFormat - lets you to choose many preset table formatting options.

1. AutoSum - helps you to add the contents of a cluster of adjacent cells.
2. List AutoFill - automatically extends cell formatting when a new item is added to the end of a list.
3. AutoShapes toolbar- will allow you to draw a number of geometrical shapes, arrows, flowchart elements, stars and more. With these shapes you can draw your own graphs.
4. Drag and Drop - feature will help you to reposition the data and text by simply
5. dragging the data with the help of mouse.
6. Charts - features will help you in presenting a graphical representation of your data in the form of Pie, Bar, Line charts and more.
7. PivotTable - flips and sums data in seconds and allows you to perform data analysis and generating reports like periodic financial statements, statistical reports, etc. You can also analyse complex data relationships graphically.
8. Shortcut Menus - commands that are appropriate to the task that you are doing appear by clicking the right mouse button.

WHAT IS A DATABASE?

A database is information that is set up for easy access, management and updating. Computer databases typically store aggregations of data records or files that contain information, such as sales transactions, customer data, financials and product information.

Databases are used for storing, maintaining and accessing any sort of data. They collect information on people, places or things. That information is gathered in one place so that it can be observed and analyzed. Databases can be thought of as an organized collection of information.

What are databases used for?

Businesses use data stored in databases to make informed business decisions. Some of the ways organizations use databases include the following:

- **Improve business processes.** Companies collect data about business processes, such sales, order processing and customer service. They analyze that data to improve these processes, expand their business and grow revenue.
- **Keep track of customers.** Databases often store information about people, such as customers or users. For example, social media platforms use databases to store user information, such as names, email addresses and user behavior. The data is used to recommend content to users and improve the user experience.
- **Secure personal health information.** Healthcare providers use databases to securely store personal health data to inform and improve patient care.
- **Store personal data.** Databases can also be used to store personal information. For example, personal cloud storage is available for individual users to store media, such as photos, in a managed cloud.

Evolution of databases

Databases were first created in the 1960s. These early databases were network models where each record is related to many primary and secondary records. Hierarchical databases were also among the early models. They have tree schemas with a root directory of records linked to several subdirectories.

E.F. Codd created the relational database while at IBM. It became the standard for database systems because of its logical schema, or the way it is organized. The use of a logical schema separates the relational database from physical storage.

The relational database, combined with the growth of the internet beginning in the mid-1990s, led to a proliferation of databases. Many business and consumer applications rely on databases.

Types of databases

There are many types of databases. They may be classified according to content type: bibliographic, full text, numeric and images. In computing, databases are often classified based on the organizational approach they use.

Some of the main organizational databases include the following:

Relational. This tabular approach defines data so it can be reorganized and accessed in many ways. Relational databases are comprised of tables. Data is placed into predefined categories in those tables. Each table has columns with at least one data category, and rows that have a certain data instance for the categories which are defined in the columns. Information in a relational database about a specific customer is organized into rows, columns and tables. These are indexed to make it easier to search using SQL or NoSQL queries.

Relational databases use SQL in their user and application program interfaces. A new data category can easily be added to a relational database without having to change the existing applications. A relational database management system (RDBMS) is used to store, manage, query and retrieve data in a relational database.

Typically, the RDBMS gives users the ability to control read/write access, specify report generation and analyze use. Some databases offer atomicity, consistency, isolation and durability, or ACID, compliance to guarantee that data is consistent and that transactions are complete.

Distributed. This database stores records or files in several physical locations. Data processing is also spread out and replicated across different parts of the network.

Distributed databases can be homogeneous, where all physical locations have the same underlying hardware and run the same operating systems and database applications. They can also be heterogeneous. In those cases, the hardware, OS and database applications can be different in the various locations.

Cloud. These databases are built in a public, private or hybrid cloud for a virtualized environment. Users are charged based on how much storage and bandwidth they use. They also get scalability on demand and high availability. These databases can work with applications deployed as software as a service.

NoSQL. NoSQL databases are good when dealing with large collections of distributed data. They can address big data performance issues better than relational databases. They also do well analyzing large unstructured data sets and data on virtual servers in the cloud. These databases can also be called non-relational databases.

Object-oriented. These databases hold data created using object-oriented programming languages. They focus on organizing objects rather than actions and data rather than logic. For instance, an image data record would be a data object, rather than an alphanumeric value.

Graph. These databases are a type of NoSQL database. They store, map and query relationships using concepts from graph theory. Graph databases are made up of nodes and edges. Nodes are entities and connect the nodes.

These databases are often used to analyze interconnections. Graph databases are often used to analyze data about customers as they interact with a business on webpages and in social media.

Graph databases use SPARQL, a declarative programming language and protocol, for analytics. SPARQL can perform all the analytics that SQL can perform, and can also be used for semantic analysis, or the examination of relationships. This makes it useful for performing analytics on data sets that have both structured and unstructured data. SPARQL lets users perform analytics on information stored in a relational database, as well as friend-of-a-friend relationships, PageRank and shortest path.

What are the components of a database?

While the different types of databases vary in schema, data structure and data types most suited to them, they are all comprised of the same five basic components.

1. **Hardware.** This is the physical device that database software runs on. Database hardware includes computers, servers and hard drives.
2. **Software.** Database software or application gives users control of the database. Database management system (DBMS) software is used to manage and control databases.
3. **Data.** This is the raw information that the database stores. Database administrators organize the data to make it more meaningful.
4. **Data access language.** This is the programming language that controls the database. The programming language and the DBMS must work together. One of the most common database languages is SQL.
5. **Procedures.** These rules determine how the database works and how it handles the data.

What are database challenges?

Setting up, operating and maintaining a database has some common challenges, such as the following:

- **Data security** is required because data is a valuable business asset. Protecting data stores requires skilled cybersecurity staff, which can be costly.
- **Data integrity** ensures data is trustworthy. It is not always easy to achieve data integrity because it means restricting access to databases to only those qualified to handle it.
- **Database performance** requires regular database updates and maintenance. Without the proper support, database functionality can decline as the technology supporting the database changes or as the data it contains changes.

- **Database integration** can also be difficult. It can involve integrating data sources from varying types of databases and structures into a single database or into data lakes and data warehouses.

What is a database management system?

A DBMS enables users to create and manage a database. It also helps users create, read, update and delete data in a database, and it assists with logging and auditing functions.

The DBMS provides physical and logical independence from data. Users and applications do not need to know either the physical or logical locations of data. A DBMS can also limit and control access to the database and provide different views of the same database schema to multiple users.

TOP 20 CYBER SECURITY TOOLS

Cyber Security has become a top priority among organizations due to the amount of confidential data and financial records they have flowing into their systems regularly. The regular need for technology to carry out almost every single task has resulted in the proliferation of cybercrimes. Here, we will come across the Cyber Security tools list consisting of numerous tools, which are paid, free, or open-source, that allow a cyber security analyst to maintain the company's data privacy and prevent all sorts of compromised data, financial loss, etc.

In this blog on tools used in Cyber Security, we will read in detail about the following topics:

- Types of Cyber Security Tools
- Kali Linux
- Cain and Abel
- Metasploit
- John the Ripper
- Wireshark
- Nikto
- Tcpdump
- KisMAC
- NetStumbler
- Splunk
- Forcepoint
- Aircrack-ng
- Nexpose
- Nagios
- KeePass
- Burp Suite
- POF
- Paros Proxy
- Nmap
- Nessus Professional

- Master a Cyber Security Tool

These are the numerous tools in Cyber Security that allow professionals to protect their systems and organizations from any attacks.

Types of Cyber Security Tools

Cyber Security tools can largely be divided into a number of categories. The categories in which these tools can be classified are listed below:

- Penetration testing
- Packet sniffers
- Encryption
- Scanning web vulnerability
- Network defenses
- Network security monitoring
- Detecting network intrusions

1. Kali Linux

Kali Linux is among the most common tools used in Cyber Security. This operating system consists of a range of tools that are useful in security auditing, network and system scanning for vulnerabilities, etc.

One of the main advantages of this platform is that Cyber Security experts with different levels of understanding can use it, making it an ideal choice even for entry-level professionals. Besides, a lot of the tools offered by Kali Linux are easily executable, allowing users to monitor the company's network security systems using a single click.

2. Cain and Abel

Cain and Abel are one the oldest and best Cyber Security tools that help in identifying the weaknesses in Windows and password recovery. It allows Cyber Security experts to find vulnerabilities in the password security of various systems that run on Windows.

Among its numerous functionalities, the significant ones include its ability to keep a record of VoIP communications and analyze routing protocols to figure out if the routed data packets can get compromised. This free tool for Cyber Security can disclose password boxes and cached passwords, etc., while also being capable of using force attacks that help in cracking encrypted passwords. Further, it helps in decoding passwords that are scrambled.

3. Metasploit

Metasploit has an excellent collection of tools that are perfect for penetration testing. Professionals often use it to meet a range of security objectives, such as discovering vulnerabilities of systems and networks, designing strategies to improve the company's Cyber Security defenses, and more.

Metasploit enables experts to test system security of online and web-based applications, servers, networks, etc. One of the advantages of this software is that it can uncover even emerging weaknesses and provide top-notch security round the clock.

4. John the Ripper

Security experts use John the Ripper to test the strength of passwords. Its design helps in exposing weak passwords that pose security threats to a particular system. In the beginning, it was only designed for the UNIX platform, but the new versions allow it to work on other operating systems as well, such as DOS, Windows, OpenVMS systems, etc.

John the Ripper searches for complex ciphers, encrypted login credentials, and hash-like passwords to find any weak password. This tool is developed and updated regularly to make sure that it offers accurate results during penetration testing. It is among the most ideal choices of Cyber Security experts to enhance password security.

5. Wireshark

Wireshark was earlier called Ethereal. It is among the best tools for Cyber Security, based on the console. It is a packet sniffer tool that allows professionals to analyze network protocols and sniff real-time networks in search of any vulnerabilities that can be exploited. Moreover, it collects necessary information related to the levels of network traffic.

Cyber Security professionals use this tool to store data packets and to identify the behavior and characteristics that each packet exhibits. This knowledge helps in identifying the weakness of network security. It basically keeps an eye on the network packets and presents them in a readable format. It is one of the best Cyber Security open-source tools available.

6. Nikto

Nikto is an open-source software tool used in Cyber Security to determine vulnerabilities in the web and take necessary actions. Professionals use this tool to scan for identifying and managing web vulnerabilities. Nikto's database consists of approximately 6,400 distinct types of security threats. The database offers the threat data that can be used to compare with the web vulnerability scan result. This scan covers both web servers and networks.

This tool is updated continuously, allowing users to recognize new web vulnerabilities easily. Besides, various plugins are created regularly to make them compatible with different systems.

7. Tcpdump

Tcpdump is a useful packet sniffing tool for networks. It helps in monitoring and logging TCP/IP traffic that is shared over a network. This command-based software tool analyzes the traffic of the systems, along with the network that the traffic goes through. Besides, this tool tests the network security by segregating TCP/IP data traffic received via the Internet. Tcpdump also defines the contents of the network traffic packets.

8. KisMAC

KisMAC is specifically created for providing wireless network security in MAC operating systems. This network-defined tool has numerous high-end features that are geared to be used by experts in the field, so it may not be the best choice of tool for freshers and entry-level security professionals.

KisMAC scans wireless networks that are supported on Wi-Fi cards, like Airport. It uses brute force attacks, weak scheduling, exploiting flaws, and many similar techniques to get into the security of WEP and WPA keys. If experts are able to crack them, it suggests that the keys are not secure enough, making the network vulnerable to possible cyberattacks.

9. NetStumbler

NetStumbler is a popular Cyber Security tool created for systems that run on the Windows operating system. It enables IT and Cyber Security experts to recognize open network ports and is extremely useful for the purpose of wardriving. Since it is specifically designed to run on Windows, it has no allocation for source codes. While looking for open-source network ports, it uses WAP-seeking methods unlike other tools in Cyber Security, which has made it popular among organizations for network defense.

10. Splunk

Splunk is a system security tool known due to its versatility and speed. It is one of the best tools to monitor network security. Splunk is used to conduct real-time network analysis and perform historical searches to look for threat data. This user-friendly tool is equipped with a unified user interface, along with numerous functionalities and techniques that help in the process of searching for required information.

It is an all-rounded system security tool that is also used to gather, store, and index data in repositories to generate real-time alerts, reports, visualizations, graphs, and dashboards.

11. Forcepoint

Forcepoint is a security tool, primarily meant for cloud users, that allows experts to customize SD-Wan to restrict users from being able to access certain resource data. This customization also allows them to block intrusions and probable exploitation of vulnerabilities.

This tool helps Network Admins to detect malicious acts in a network easily, giving them enough time to take necessary actions to prevent them. This is one of the significant benefits of Forcepoint over other tools as they are designed to track the problems so that users can apply the required techniques to fix them later. One of its significant functionalities in the cloud is that it warns or blocks cloud servers that pose security risks to the systems. Further, it offers a high level of security in other applications with significant data.

12. Aircrack-ng

This tool consists of numerous methods that help in analyzing the vulnerabilities of Wi-Fi security. Experts use Aircrack-ng to gather data packets connected through a network for the process of continuous monitoring. Moreover, it enables Cyber Security professionals to use its functions to export these data packets to understandable text files that can go through various security assessments.

Aircrack-ng also supports capture and injection that are crucial in terms of assessing network cards' performance. Moreover, it tests how reliable the WEP and WPA-PSK keys are by cracking them and helps an organization understand the strength of the network. This is the perfect tool to enhance and improve the network security of an organization.

13. Nexpose

Nexpose offers real-time functionalities to security professionals to scan and manage weaknesses in on-premises systems. It allows experts to find weaknesses in the systems and use that knowledge to identify and minimize the possible attacks.

Moreover, Nexpose offers a live view of various network activities to the security team. It refreshes its database regularly so that it can adapt to various types of threat environments in software and data, ensuring that the tool has the latest threat data. Also, professionals in Cyber Security can use Nexpose to assign risk scores to the weaknesses it finds, creating a priority list based on security levels.

14. Nagios

Nagios allows security professionals to efficiently monitor various networks, such as NNTP, POP3, SMTP, HTTP, ICMP, and more. Moreover, it monitors the connected systems and hosts in real time. As soon as it detects a security issue or intrusion in the network, it sends out an alert to users to warn them of the same. Here, the users have the option to choose the notification alerts that they wish to get and the ones they do not.

15. KeePass

Professionals in IT Security often use KeePass for the purpose of identity management. It allows users to use a master password to access all of their accounts they use for work. It combines security and convenience, which gives it an edge over the other Cyber Security tools for identity management.

There are numerous network and system breaches that are caused due to inaccurate password management, but this possibility is also eliminated by KeePass. This Application Software is used in companies and offices as it can help security experts to find possible risks that are caused due to human elements.

16. Burp Suite

Burp Suite is a robust tool used in the field of Cyber Security that allows organizations to enhance their network security. Security experts use Burp Suite to perform real-time scans on systems focusing on identifying vital vulnerabilities that can have a large impact on the company's security. Moreover, it simulates attacks to find the different ways in which these threats can weaken and compromise the security of the network.

Burp Suite has three versions, namely, Community, Professional, and Enterprise. The Community version of Burp Suite is available for free, but a lot of features are restricted and cannot be used in this version. It only offers the essential manual tools. The Professional and Enterprise versions of Burp Suite are for commercial use, and hence, they are not available for free use. Though it can be a little expensive for small companies, Burp Suite is among the top choices of security tools for most organizations.

17. POf

POf is a widely adopted Cyber Security tool that enables companies to monitor networks, regardless of any updates released by developers for a while. The tool does not create any extra data traffic while monitoring the network, making it an efficient network security tool. It is used by professionals to depict the host operating systems that are connected to a network.

POf allows Cyber Security professionals to perform a range of functionalities, such as building name lookups, assorted queries, probes, etc. Its quick and lightweight nature has made it popular among Cyber Security specialists with advanced skills, but not among beginners as they may find it difficult to learn and use the tool.

18. Paros Proxy

Paros Proxy is a Java-based security tool comprising a set of useful tools that allow experts to perform several security tests that lead to the discovery of various vulnerabilities in the web. Web spiders, vulnerability scanners, and the traffic recorded to retain real-time network activities are some of the significant tools available in Paros Proxy. Moreover, it enables experts to identify network intrusions.

Paros Proxy also helps in uncovering basic and popular Cyber Security threats, including SQL injection attacks and cross-site scripting. Besides, one of its main benefits is that it can easily be edited with the help of rudimentary Java or HTTP/HTTPS. In simple terms, Paros Proxy is an ideal tool to find network vulnerabilities before cyber attackers and hackers exploit them to cause breaches.

19. Nmap

Nmap is otherwise called Network Mapper. It is a free and open-source tool in Cyber Security that can help in scanning IT systems and networks to recognize security vulnerabilities. Further, it enables professionals to map out possible areas of attacks on the network, monitor host uptime and service, and take significant security measures accordingly.

Nmap can run on almost all popular operating systems, which makes it a preferred tool among professionals. Apart from that, it allows experts to scan for vulnerabilities on the web, irrespective of the size of the network. Also, it provides the IT professionals with an overview of the characteristics of the network, such as the types of packet filters and firewalls deployed to keep the network secure, the hosts that are connected to the network, the operating system it runs on, etc.

20. Nessus Professional

This tool helps organizations improve network integrity and rectify numerous flaws, including misconfiguration of the security settings, implementing incorrect security patches, and many other mistakes. Besides, Nessus Professional allows professionals to find weaknesses in the network, such as software bugs, incorrect security configurations in operating systems, IT devices, and software applications, missing and incomplete patches, etc., and manage them as required.

The Nessus Pro version enables security experts to utilize its free vulnerability scanner that helps in finding possible threats and exploits. Besides, one of its main benefits is that its database is regularly updated with the new and updated threat data, allowing it to contain the latest details regarding the vulnerabilities found on the network.

Master a Cyber Security Tool

In this 'Top 20 Cyber Security Tools to Look out for in 2021' blog, you have read in-depth about some of the most popular and commonly used tools in the field of Cyber Security. If you are aspiring to become a professional in this field, then it is important that you not only get trained in it but learn to use some of these tools to gain a competitive edge while applying for jobs. This list of tools aims to help you choose those that are best suited for your experience and career. Get started!

WHAT IS COMPUTER VIRUS?

A computer virus is a type of malware that attaches to another program (like a document), which can replicate and spread after a person first runs it on their system. For instance, you could receive an email with a malicious attachment, open the file unknowingly, and then the computer virus runs on your computer. Viruses are harmful and can destroy data, slow down system resources, and log keystrokes.

Cybercriminals aren't creating new viruses all the time, instead they focus their efforts on more sophisticated and lucrative threats. When people talk about "getting a virus" on their computer, they usually mean some form of malware—it could be a virus, computer worm, Trojan, ransomware or some other harmful thing. Viruses and malware continue to evolve, and often cybercriminals use the type that gives them the best return at that particular time.

Virus vs. malware - what is the difference?

The terms "virus" and "malware" are often used interchangeably, but they're not the same thing. While a computer virus is a type of malware, not all malware are computer viruses.

The easiest way to differentiate computer viruses from other forms of malware is to think about viruses in biological terms. Take the flu virus, for example. The flu requires some kind of interaction between two people—like a hand shake, a kiss, or touching something an infected person touched. Once the flu virus gets inside a person's system it attaches to healthy human cells, using those cells to create more viral cells.

A computer virus works in much the same way:

1. A computer virus requires a host program.
2. A computer virus requires user action to transmit from one system to another.
3. A computer virus attaches bits of its own malicious code to other files or replaces files outright with copies of itself.

It's that second virus trait that tends to confuse people. Viruses can't spread without some sort of action from a user, like opening up an infected Word document. Worms, on the other hand, are able to spread across systems and networks on their own, making them much more prevalent and dangerous.

Famously, the 2017 WannaCry ransomware worm spread around the world, took down thousands of Windows systems, and raked in an appreciable amount of untraceable Bitcoin ransom payments for the alleged North Korean attackers.

Computer viruses don't typically capture headlines like that—at least not anymore. They are still a harmful type of malware, but they are not the only type of threat out there today, on your computer or mobile device.

Windows, Mac, Android, and iOS

Many computer viruses target systems running Microsoft Windows. Macs, on the other hand, have enjoyed a reputation as virus-proof super machines, but in Apple's own admission, Macs do get malware. There are more Windows users in the world than Mac users and cybercriminals simply choose to write viruses for the operating system (OS) with the largest amount of potential victims.

Today, the "computer" in our pockets may be the one we use most often: our smartphones. Android and iOS are susceptible to various forms of malware, too. Fortunately, most cybersecurity companies like Malwarebytes offer protection for Windows, Mac, Android, and iOS today.

Computer virus examples

Sometimes to understand what something is, we have to examine what it isn't. Keeping that in mind, let's play: Is It a Virus ?

In the Is It a Virus game we're going to take a look at examples of things people on the Internet commonly believe to be a virus and explain why it is or isn't. What fun!

Is a Trojan a virus

? Trojans can be viruses. A Trojan is a computer program pretending to be something it's not for the purposes of sneaking onto your computer and delivering some sort of malware. To put it another way, if a virus disguises itself then it's a Trojan. A Trojan could be a seemingly benign file downloaded off the web or a Word doc attached to an email. Think that movie you downloaded from your favorite P2P sharing site is safe? What about that "important" tax document from your accountant? Think twice, because they could contain a virus.

Is a worm a virus ? Worms are not viruses, though the terms are sometimes used interchangeably. Even worse, the terms are sometimes used together in a strange and contradictory word salad; i.e. a "worm virus malware." It's either a worm or a virus, but it can't be both, because worms and viruses refer to two similar but different threats. As mentioned earlier, a virus needs a host system to replicate and some sort of action from a user to spread from one system to the next. A worm, conversely, doesn't need a host system and is capable of spreading across a network and any systems connected to the network without user action. Once on a system, worms are known to drop malware (often ransomware) or open a backdoor.

Is ransomware a virus ? Ransomware can be a virus. Does the virus prevent victims from accessing their system or personal files and demands ransom payment in order to regain access à la ransomware? If so, then it's a ransomware virus. In fact, the very first ransomware was a virus (more on that later). Nowadays, most ransomware comes as a result of computer worm, capable of spreading from one system to the next and across networks without user action (e.g. WannaCry).

Is a rootkit a virus ? Rootkits are not viruses. A rootkit is a software package designed to give attackers "root" access or admin access to a given system. Crucially, rootkits cannot self-replicate and don't spread across systems.

Is a software bug a virus ? Software bugs are not viruses. Even though we sometimes refer to a biological virus as a "bug" (e.g. "I caught a stomach bug"), software bugs and viruses are not the same thing. A software bug refers to a flaw or mistake in the computer code that a given software program is made up of. Software bugs can cause programs to behave in ways the software manufacturer never intended. The Y2K bug famously caused programs to display the wrong date, because the programs could only manage dates through the year 1999. After 1999 the year rolled over like the odometer on an old car to 1900. While the Y2K bug was relatively harmless, some software bugs can pose a serious threat to consumers. Cybercriminals can take advantage of bugs in order to gain unauthorized access to a system for the purposes of dropping malware, stealing private information, or opening up a backdoor. This is known as an exploit.

How do I prevent computer viruses?

Preventing computer viruses from infecting your computer starts with situational awareness.

"Situational awareness is something law enforcement and militaries have practiced for decades. It refers to a police officer or a soldier's ability to perceive threats and make the best decision possible in a potentially stressful situation," said Malwarebytes Head of Security, John Donovan.

"As it applies to cybersecurity, situational awareness is your first line of defense against cyberthreats. By staying on the lookout for phishing attacks and avoiding suspicious links and attachments, consumers can largely avoid most malware threats."

Regarding email attachments and embedded links, even if the sender is someone you know: viruses have been known to hijack Outlook contact lists on infected computers and send virus laden attachments to friends, family and coworkers, the Melissa virus being a perfect example.

If an email reads oddly, it's probably a phishing scam or malspam. When in doubt about the authenticity of an email, don't be afraid to reach out to the sender. A simple call or text message can save you a lot of trouble.

Next, invest in good cybersecurity software. We've made a distinction between computer viruses and malware, which now begs the question, "Do I need antivirus software or anti-malware software?" We've covered this topic before in great detail so checkout our article on antivirus vs. anti-malware. For now, though, here's a quick gloss on the subject.

Antivirus (AV) refers to early forms of cybersecurity software focused on stopping computer viruses. Just viruses. Anti-malware refers to all-encompassing threat protection designed to stop old-fashioned viruses as well as today's malware threats.

Given a choice between traditional AV with limited threat detection technology and modern anti-malware with all the bells and whistles, invest in anti-malware and rest easy at night.

As mentioned previously in this piece, traditional AV solutions rely on signature-based detection. AV scans your computer and compares each and every file against a database of known viruses that functions a lot like a criminal database. If there's a signature match, the malicious file is thrown into virus jail before it can cause any damage.

The problem with signature-based detection is that it can't stop what's known as a zero-day virus; that is, a virus that cybersecurity researchers have never seen before and for which there is no criminal profile. Until the zero-day virus is added to the database, traditional AV can't detect it.

Malwarebytes' Multi-Vector Protection, conversely, combines several forms of threat detection technology into one malware crushing machine. Amongst these many layers of protection, Malwarebytes uses what's called heuristic analysis to look for telltale malicious behavior from any given program. If it looks like a virus and behaves like a virus, then it's probably a virus.

Use a VPN to protect your privacy online, especially when you're on the public Wi-Fi network. A VPN app hides your IP address and tunnels your traffic through a secure connection. Read more about VPN here - What is VPN.

How do I remove computer viruses ?

Going back to our virus analogy one final time—removing a virus from your body requires a healthy immune system. Same for your computer. A good anti-malware program is like having a healthy immune system. As your immune system moves through your body looking for and killing off invading viral cells, anti-malware scans for files and malicious code that don't belong on your system and gets rid of them.

The free version of Malwarebytes is a good place to start if you know or suspect your computer has a virus. Available for Windows and Mac, the free version of Malwarebytes will scan for malware infections and clean them up after the fact. Get a free premium trial of Malwarebytes for Windows or Malwarebytes for Mac to stop infections before they start. You can also try our Android and iOS apps free to protect your smartphones and tablets.

News on computer viruses

- Barcode Scanner app on Google Play infects 10 million users with one update
- 'Just tell me how to fix my computer:' a crash course on malware detection
- Do Chromebooks need antivirus protection?
- Scammers use old browser trick to create fake virus download
- Our computers, ourselves: digital vs. biological security
- Malware vs. virus: What's the difference?

History of computer viruses

Today's malware authors owe a lot to the cybercriminals of yesteryear. All the tactics and techniques employed by cybercriminals creating modern malware were first seen in early viruses. Things like Trojans, ransomware, and polymorphic code. These all came from early computer viruses. To understand the threat landscape of today, we need to peer back through time and look at the viruses of yesteryear.

1949, John von Neumann and "self-reproducing machines"

It was in those salad days of computing that mathematician, engineer, and polymath John von Neumann delivered a lecture on the Theory and Organization of Complicated Automata in which he first argued that computer programs could "self-reproduce." In an era where computers were the size of houses, and programs were stored on mile-long punch tapes, Neumann's ideas must've sounded like something from a sci-fi pulp novel.

1982, The proto computer-virus

In 1982 a fifteen-year-old boy pranking his friends proved Neumann's theory a reality. Rich Skrenta's Elk Cloner is widely regarded as the first proto-computer virus (the term "computer virus" didn't exist just yet). Elk Cloner targeted Apple II computers, causing infected machines to display a poem from Skrenta:

1984, Computer virus, defined

In 1984 computer scientist Fred Cohen handed in his graduate thesis paper, Computer Viruses – Theory and Experiments in which he coined the term "computer virus," which is great because "complicated self-reproducing automata" is a real mouthful. In the same paper, Cohen also gave us our first definition of "computer virus" as "a program that can 'infect' other programs by modifying them to include a possibly evolved copy of itself."

1984, Core War

Up to this point, most talk about computer viruses happened only in the rarified air of college campuses and research labs. But a 1984 Scientific American article let the virus out of the lab. In the piece, author and computer scientist A.K. Dewdney shared the details of an exciting new computer game of his creation called Core War. In the game, computer programs vie for control of a virtual computer. The game was essentially a battle arena where computer programmers could pit their viral creations against each other. For two dollars Dewdney would send detailed instructions for setting up your own Core War battles within the confines of a virtual computer. What would happen if a battle program was taken out of the virtual computer and placed on a real computer system? In a follow-up article for Scientific American, Dewdney shared a letter from two Italian readers who were inspired by their experience with Core War to create a real virus on the Apple II. It's not a stretch to think other readers were similarly inspired.

1986, the first PC virus

The Brain virus was the first to target Microsoft's text-based Windows precursor, MS-DOS. The brainchild of Pakistani brothers and software engineers, Basit and Amjad Farooq, Brain acted like an early form of copyright protection, stopping people from pirating their heart monitoring software. If the target system contained a pirated version of the brother's software, the "victim" would receive the on-screen message, "WELCOME TO THE DUNGEON . . . CONTACT US FOR VACCINATION" along with the brothers' names, phone number, and business address in Pakistan. Other than guilt tripping victims in to paying for their pirated software, Brain had no harmful effects.

Speaking with F-Secure, Basit called Brain a "very friendly virus." Amjad added that today's viruses, the descendants of Brain, are "a purely criminal act."

1986, Viruses go into stealth mode

Also in 1986, the BHP virus was the first to target the Commodore 64 computer. Infected computers displayed a text message with the names of the multiple hackers who created the virus—the digital equivalent of scrawling "(your name) was here" on the side of a building. BHP also has the distinction of being the first stealth virus; that is, a virus that avoids detection by hiding the changes it makes to a target system and its files.

1988, Computer virus of the year

1988, one could argue, was the year computer viruses went mainstream. In September of that year, a story on computer viruses appeared on the cover of TIME magazine. The cover image depicted viruses as cute, googly eyed cartoon insects crawling all over a desktop computer. Up to this point, computer viruses were relatively harmless. Yes, they were annoying, but not destructive. So how did computer viruses go from nuisance threat to system destroying plague?

1988, front page of The New York Times

A little over a month after the TIME magazine piece, a story about the "most serious computer 'virus' attack" in US history appeared on the front page of The New York Times. It was Robert Tappan Morris' Internet worm, erroneously referred to as a "virus." In all fairness, no one knew what a worm was. Morris's creation was the archetype. The Morris worm knocked out more than 6,000 computers as it spread across the ARPANET, a government operated early version of the Internet restricted to schools and military installations. The Morris worm was the first known use of a dictionary attack. As the name suggests, a dictionary attack involves taking a list of words and using it to try and guess the username and password combination of a target system.

Robert Morris was the first person charged under the newly enacted Computer Fraud and Abuse Act, which made it illegal to mess with government and financial systems, and any computer that contributes to US commerce and communications. In his defense, Morris never intended his namesake worm to cause so much damage. According to Morris, the worm was designed to test security flaws and estimate the size of the early Internet. A bug caused the worm to infect targeted systems over and over again, with each subsequent infection consuming processing power until the system crashed.

1989, Computer viruses go viral

In 1989 the AIDS Trojan was the first example of what would later come to be known as ransomware. Victims received a 5.25-inch floppy disk in the mail labelled "AIDS Information" containing a simple questionnaire designed to help recipients figure out if they were at risk for the AIDS virus (thc biological one).

While an apt (albeit insensitive) metaphor, there's no indication the virus' creator, Dr. Joseph L. Popp, intended to draw parallels between his digital creation and the deadly AIDS virus. Many of the 20,000 disk recipients, Medium reported, were delegates for the World Health Organization (WHO). The WHO previously rejected Popp for an AIDS research position.

Loading thc questionnairc infcctcd target systems with the AIDS Trojan. The AIDS Trojan would then lay dormant for the next 89 boot ups. When victims started their computer for thc 90th timc, thcy'd be presented with an on-screen message ostensibly from "PC Cyborg Corporation" demanding payment for "your software lease," similar to the Brain virus from three years earlier. Unlike the Brain virus, however, the AIDS Trojan encrypted the victims' files.

In an era before Bitcoin and other untraceable cryptocurrencies, victims had to send ransom funds to a PO box in Panama in order to receive the decryption software and regain access to their files. Funds, Popp claimed after his arrest, were destined for AIDS virus research.

1990s, Rise of the Internet

By 1990 ARPANET was decommissioned in favor of its public, commercially accessible cousin the Internet. And thanks to Tim Berners-Lee's pioneering work on web browsers and web pages, the Internet was now a user-friendly place anyone could explore without special technical knowledge. There were 2.6 million users on the Internet in 1990, according to Our World in Data. By the end of the decade, that number would surpass 400 million.

HACKING DEFINITION: WHAT IS HACKING?

Hacking refers to activities that seek to compromise digital devices, such as computers, smartphones, tablets, and even entire networks. And while hacking might not always be for malicious purposes, nowadays most references to hacking, and hackers, characterize it/them as unlawful activity by cybercriminals—motivated by financial gain, protest, information gathering (spying), and even just for the "fun" of the challenge.

Who are hackers?

Many think that "hacker" refers to some self-taught whiz kid or rogue programmer skilled at modifying computer hardware or software so it can be used in ways outside the original developers' intent. But this is a narrow view that doesn't begin to encompass the wide range of reasons why someone turns to hacking. Is all hacking bad? Check out this video which will give you some ideas about different types of hacking:

Hacking tools: How do hackers hack?

Hacking is typically technical in nature (like creating malvertising that deposits malware in a drive-by attack requiring no user interaction). But hackers can also use psychology to trick the user into clicking on a malicious attachment or providing personal data. These tactics are referred to as "social engineering."

In fact, it's accurate to characterize hacking as an over-arching umbrella term for activity behind most if not all of the malware and malicious cyberattacks on the computing public, businesses, and governments. Besides social engineering and malvertising, common hacking techniques include:

- Botnets
- Browser hijacks
- Denial of service (DDoS) attacks
- Ransomware
- Rootkits

- Trojans
- Viruses
- Worms

From script kiddies to organized cybercrime

As such, hacking has evolved from teenage mischief into a billion-dollar growth business, whose adherents have established a criminal infrastructure that develops and sells turnkey hacking tools to would-be crooks with less sophisticated technical skills (known as "script kiddies"). As an example, see: Emotet.

In another example, Windows users are reportedly the target of a wide-spread cybercriminal effort offering remote access to IT systems for just $10 via a dark web hacking store—potentially enabling attackers to steal information, disrupt systems, deploy ransomware, and more. Systems advertised for sale on the forum range from Windows XP through to Windows 10. The storeowners even offer tips for how those using the illicit logins can remain undetected.

"Hacking has evolved from teenage mischief into a billion-dollar growth business."

Types of hacking/hackers

Broadly speaking, you can say that hackers attempt to break into computers and networks for any of four reasons.

- There's criminal financial gain, meaning the theft of credit card numbers or defrauding banking systems.
- Next, gaining street cred and burnishing one's reputation within hacker subculture motivates some hackers as they leave their mark on websites they vandalize as proof that they pulled off the hack.
- Then there's corporate espionage or cyber espionage, when one company's hackers seek to steal information on a competitor's products and services to gain a marketplace advantage.

- Finally, entire nations engage in state-sponsored hacking to steal business and/or national intelligence, to destabilize their adversaries' infrastructure, or even to sow discord and confusion in the target country. (There's consensus that China and Russia have carried out such attacks, including one on Forbes.com. In addition, the recent attacks on the Democratic National Committee [DNC] made the news in a big way—especially after Microsoft says hackers accused of hacking into the Democratic National Committee have exploited previously undisclosed flaws in Microsoft's Windows operating system and Adobe Systems' Flash software. There are also instances of hacking courtesy of the United States government.)

There's even another category of cybercriminals: the hacker who is politically or socially motivated for some cause. Such hacker-activists, or "hacktivists," strive to focus public attention on an issue by garnering unflattering attention on the target—usually by making sensitive information public. For notable hacktivist groups, along with some of their more famous undertakings, see Anonymous, WikiLeaks, and LulzSec.

Hacking news

- Hackers take over 1.1 million accounts by trying reused passwords
- Podcast: Hackers, tractors, and a few delayed actors. How hacker Sick Codes learned too much about John Deere
- The Olympics: a timeline of scams, hacks, and malware
- North Korean hackers charged with $1.3 billion of cyberheists
- Credit card skimmer piggybacks on Magento 1 hacking spree
- Misleading cybersecurity lessons from pop culture: how Hollywood teaches to hack
- Video game portrayals of hacking: NITE Team 4
- Hacking with AWS: incorporating leaky buckets into your OSINT workflow

Ethical hacking? White, black, and grey hats

There's also another way we parse hackers. Remember the classic old Western movies? Good guys = white hats. Bad guys = black hats. Today's cybersecurity frontier retains that Wild West vibe, with white hat and black hat hackers, and even a third in-between category.

If a hacker is a person with deep understanding of computer systems and software, and who uses that knowledge to somehow subvert that technology, then a black hat hacker does so for stealing something valuable or other malicious reasons. So it's reasonable to assign any of those four motivations (theft, reputation, corporate espionage, and nation-state hacking) to the black hats.

White hat hackers, on the other hand, strive to improve the security of an organization's security systems by finding vulnerable flaws so that they can prevent identity theft or other cybercrimes before the black hats notice. Corporations even employ their own white hat hackers as part of their support staff, as a recent article from the New York Times online edition highlights. Or businesses can even outsource their white hat hacking to services such as HackerOne, which tests software products for vulnerabilities and bugs for a bounty.

Finally, there's the gray hat crowd, hackers who use their skills to break into systems and networks without permission (just like the black hats). But instead of wreaking criminal havoc, they might report their discovery to the target owner and offer to repair the vulnerability for a small fee.

Hacking prevention

If your computer, tablet, or phone is at the bull's-eye of the hacker's target, then surround it with concentric rings of precautions.

Anti-malware protection

First and foremost, download a reliable anti-malware product (or app for the phone), which can both detect and neutralize malware and block connections to malicious phishing websites. Of course, whether you're on Windows, Android, a Mac, an iPhone, or in a business network, we recommend the layered protection of Malwarebytes for Windows, Malwarebytes for Mac, Malwarebytes for Android, Malwarebytes for Chromebook, Malwarebytes for iOS, and Malwarebytes business products.

Be careful with apps

Second, only download phone apps from the legitimate marketplaces that police themselves for malware-carrying apps, such as Google Play and Amazon Appstore. (Note that Apple policy restricts iPhone users to download only from the App Store.) Even so, every time you download an app, check the ratings and reviews first. If it has a low rating and a low number of downloads, it is best to avoid that app.

Protect your info

Know that no bank or online payment system will ever ask you for your login credentials, social security number, or credit card numbers by means of email.

Update your software

Whether you're on your phone or a computer, make sure your operating system remains updated. And update your other resident software as well.

Browse carefully

Avoid visiting unsafe websites, and never download unverified attachments or click on links in unfamiliar emails. You can also use Malwarebytes Browser Guard for safer browsing.

Password safety

All the above is basic hygiene, and always a good idea. But the bad guys are forever looking for a new way into your system. If a hacker discovers one of your passwords that you use for multiple services, they have apps that can breach your other accounts. So make your passwords long and complicated, avoid using the same one for different accounts, and instead use a password manager. Because the value of even a single hacked email account can rain disaster down on you.

"Know that no bank or online payment system will ever ask you for your login credentials, social security number, or credit card numbers by means of email."

Use a VPN (Virtual Private Network)

A virtual private network, or VPN, is a technology that allows you to establish a secure and private connection to the Internet. VPN essentially acts like a digital middleman between you and the Internet. Your Internet traffic travels through an encrypted tunnel and will look like it's coming from the VPN server rather than your own IP address (what is IP address). This gives you online privacy and secures your digital footprint - which is very important especially if you are using a public Wi-Fi or a shared Wi-Fi connection.

Hacking on Android phones

While most associate hacking with Windows computers, the Android operating system also offers an inviting target for hackers.

A bit of history: Early hackers who obsessively explored low-tech methods for getting around the secure telecommunication networks (and expensive long-distance calls of their era) were originally called phreaks—a combination of the words phone and freaks. They were a defined subculture in the 1970s, and their activity was called phreaking.

Nowadays, phreakers have evolved out of the analog technology era and become hackers in the digital world of more than two billion mobile devices. Mobile phone hackers use a variety of methods to access an individual's mobile phone and intercept voicemails, phone calls, text messages, and even the phone's microphone and camera, all without that user's permission or even knowledge.

"Cybercriminals could view your stored data on the phone, including identity and financial information."

Why Android?

Compared to iPhones, Android phones are much more fractured, whose open-source nature and inconsistencies in standards in terms of software development put the Androids at a greater risk of data corruption and data theft. And any number of bad things result from Android hacking.

Cybercriminals could view your stored data on the phone, including identity and financial information. Likewise, hackers can track your location, force your phone to text premium websites, or even spread their hack (with an embedded malicious link) to others among your contacts, who will click on it because it appears to come from you.

Of course, legitimate law enforcement might hack phones with a warrant to store copies of texts and emails, transcribe private conversations, or follow the suspect's movements. But black hat hackers could definitely do harm by accessing your bank account credentials, deleting data, or adding a host of malicious programs.

Phishing

Phone hackers have the advantage of many computer hacking techniques, which are easy to adapt to Androids. Phishing, the crime of targeting individuals or members of entire organizations to lure them into revealing sensitive information through social engineering, is a tried and true method for criminals. In fact, because a phone displays a much smaller address bar compared to a PC, phishing on a mobile Internet browser probably makes it easier to counterfeit a seemingly trusted website without revealing the subtle tells (such as intentional misspellings) that you can see on a desktop browser. So you get a note from your bank asking you to log on to resolve an urgent problem, click on the conveniently provided link, enter your credentials in the form, and the hackers have you.

Trojanized apps

Trojanized apps downloaded from unsecured marketplaces are another crossover hacker threat to Androids. Major Android app stores (Google and Amazon) keep careful watch on the third-party apps; but embedded malware can get through either occasionally from the trusted sites, or more often from the sketchier ones. This is the way your phone ends up hosting adware, spyware, ransomware, or any other number of malware nasties.

Bluehacking

"Bluehacking gains access to your phone when it shows up on an unprotected Bluetooth network."

Other methods are even more sophisticated and don't require manipulating the user into clicking on a bad link. Bluehacking gains access to your phone when it shows up on an unprotected Bluetooth network. It's even possible to mimic a trusted network or cell phone tower to re-route text messages or log-on sessions. And if you leave your unlocked phone unattended in a public space, instead of just stealing it, a hacker can clone it by copying the SIM card, which is like handing over the keys to your castle.

Hacking on Macs

Lest you think that hacking is only a Windows problem, Mac users, be assured—you are not immune. In 2021, Apple publicly confirmed that yes, Macs get malware.

Previous to that admission, in 2017 there was a phishing campaign targeting Mac users, mostly in Europe. Conveyed by a Trojan that was signed with a valid Apple developer certificate, the hack phished for credentials by throwing up a full-screen alert claiming that there's an essential OS X update waiting to be installed. If the hack succeeded, the attackers gained complete access to all of the victim's communication, allowing them to eavesdrop on all web browsing, even if it's an HTTPS connection with the lock icon.

In addition to social engineering hacks on Macs, the occasional hardware flaw can also create vulnerabilities, as was the case with the so-called Meltdown and Spectre flaws that The Guardian reported in early 2018. Apple responded by developing protections against the flaw, but advised customers to download software only from trusted sources such as its iOS and Mac App Stores to help prevent hackers from being able to use the processor vulnerabilities.

And then there was the insidious Calisto, a variant of the Proton Mac malware that operated in the wild for two years before being discovered in July 2018. It was buried in a fake Mac cybersecurity installer, and, among other functions, collected usernames and passwords.

More recent examples of hacking on Macs and Mac malware include Silver Sparrow, ThiefQuest, and malware masquerading as iTerm2. From viruses to malware to security flaws, hackers have created an extensive toolkit to wreak hacker havoc on your Mac. A good Mac antivirus and anti-malware program will help defend your Mac against such malware.

How does hacking affect my business?

For criminal-minded hackers, business is booming. Ransomware attacks on major businesses have been featured heavily in the news throughout 2021. Some of these have been high-profile, such as the attacks on the Colonial Pipeline, JBS (the world's largest meatpacker), or the large ferry service Steamship Authority. There are a number of ransomware gangs, Ransomware-as-a-Service providers, and types of ransomware out in the wild. You may be familiar with names like Conti, Ryuk, or GandCrab, for example.

Trojans remain a threat to businesses, with some of the most well-known being Emotet and TrickBot. Emotet, Trickbot, and GandCrab all rely on malspam as their primary vector of infection. These malicious spam emails, disguised as familiar brands, trick your end users into clicking malicious download links or opening an attachment loaded with malware. In an interesting twist, Emotet has evolved from being a banking Trojan in its own right into a tool for delivering other malware, including other banking Trojans like Trickbot.

So what happens when cybercriminals are able to hack into your network?

Emotet, for instance, hobbled critical systems in the City of Allentown, PA, requiring help from Microsoft's incident response team to clean up. All told, the city racked up remediation costs to the tune of $1 million.

GandCrab is just as awful. It's been estimated the ransomware with the gross sounding name has already netted its authors somewhere around $300 million in paid ransoms, with individual ransoms set from $600 to $700,000.

How to protect your business from hacking

In light of the ransomware and Trojan attacks currently favored by criminal hackers, the question now is: how can I protect my business from hacking? Here's some tips for staying safe.

- Implement network segmentation. Spreading your data across smaller subnetworks reduces your exposure during an attack. This can help contain infections to only a few endpoints instead of your entire infrastructure.
- Enforce the principle of least privilege (PoLP). By only giving users the access level they need to do their jobs and nothing more you can minimize the potential damage from ransomware attacks.
- Backup all your data. This goes for all the endpoints on your network and network shares too. As long as your data is archived, you can always wipe an infected system and restore from a backup.
- Educate end users on how to spot malspam. Users should be wary of unsolicited emails and attachments from unknown senders. When handling attachments, your users should avoid executing executable files and avoid enabling macros on Office files. When in doubt, reach out. Train end users to inquire further if suspicious emails appear to be from a trusted source. One quick phone call or email goes a long way towards avoiding malware.
- Educate staff on creating strong passwords and implement some form of multi-factor authentication (MFA)—two-factor authentication at a bare minimum.
- Patch and update your software. Emotet and Trickbot rely on the Windows EternalBlue/DoublePulsar vulnerabilities to infect machines and spread across networks so keep your systems up-to-date.
- Get proactive about endpoint protection. Malwarebytes, for example, has multiple options for your business with Endpoint Protection and Endpoint Detection and Response.

TROJANS INPUT AND OUTPUT DEVICES

In general, trojans are malicious programs that can infiltrate a computer system and perform unauthorized actions. Depending on the specific type of trojan, it may be able to interfere with input and output devices.

For example, a trojan could potentially capture keystrokes or mouse clicks, allowing an attacker to monitor what a user is typing or clicking on. This could be used to steal sensitive information like passwords or credit card numbers.

Similarly, a trojan could potentially manipulate the output of a computer system, such as displaying fake error messages or redirecting a user's web browser to a malicious site.

However, it's important to note that not all trojans have these capabilities, and there are many other types of malware that can also affect input and output devices. It's always a good idea to have up-to-date security software and to be cautious when downloading and installing software from untrusted sources.

System Security
Derrick Rountree, in Security for Microsoft Windows System Administrators, 2011

Trojans
Trojans are also sometimes referred to as Trojan horses. This comes from the story of the Trojan horse in Greek mythology. The Greeks gave the Trojans the Trojan horse as a gift. The Trojans allowed the gift inside their kingdom. But inside the horse were Greek soldiers who attacked the Trojans. Computer Trojans are similar. They will either disguise themselves as useful applications or attach themselves to a useful application. This way, users will activate the Trojan without knowing they are doing any harm. Trojans, like viruses, are not self-replicating. They require user interaction to move from one system to another. Trojans are mostly used to allow attackers to gain remote access to a system. The attacker may try to copy information from the system or gain keyboard control of the system.

Online Security
Sudhanshu Chauhan, Nutan Kumar Panda, in Hacking Web Intelligence, 2015

Trojan

Trojan is quite interesting malware, it generally comes as a gift such as if we visit restricted sites then we will get some advertisements such as we won an iPhone, click here to apply and all, or in popular paid games as free, then once user is lured to that and installs that after downloading then the application will create a backdoor and provide all user actions to the attacker. So to spread a Trojan, if the attacker will choose a popular demanding paid app, game, movie or song then the chances of getting more people are quite a lot.

Trojans are nonself-replicating but hide behind another program. It is recommended that do not install any paid thing that comes as free. You never know what is hidden inside that application and also use antimalware in system for better safety.

Operating System and Device Vulnerabilities

In Mobile Malware Attacks and Defense, 2009

Palm OS Malware

There exists almost no Palm OS malware. The only three known pieces of malware are really simple and more like proof-of-concepts. However, all three are destructive so they cannot be classified as proof-of-concept.

The LibertyCrack Trojan

The LibertyCrack Trojan is a simple piece of malware that pretends to be a crack for the Liberty Gameboy Emulator. Like many Trojans, the LibertyCrack Trojan must be installed by the user. This means it also does not replace itself and therefore cannot spread. When the Trojan is run by the user, it deletes all applications (all PRC databases) and reboots the device. LibertyCrack was discovered in the summer of 2000.

The Phage Virus

Phage is the first virus created for Palm OS–based devices. It is a real virus since it is self-replicating and infects other applications installed on a device. Compared to viruses created for early personal computers, Phage is still very simple since it actually does not infect but destroys infected application binaries. The application icon is not modified in the process, thus the user only discovers the infection while trying to run an infected application. Phage was discovered in late 2000.

The Vapor Trojan

The Vapor Trojan is very similar to the Liberty Trojan. It cannot replicate and has to be installed by the user of a device. The malicious functionally of Vapor is also very similar to the Liberty Trojan but instead of deleting all applications on a device it just hides them. This is done by changing the application database attributes so the application launcher does not display them. The Vapor Trojan was also discovered in late 2000.

DVS Archiving and Storage

Anthony C. Caputo, in Digital Video Surveillance and Security (Second Edition), 2014

Malicious Software

A Trojan (derived from the Trojan horse of mythology) is a file that has hidden content with malicious intent. Trojans are typically encapsulated as something enticing, such as a game, video, or picture, appearing harmless, but once you execute (run) this file, the worm or virus is released onto the system.

Viruses are computer programs that have the sole purpose of destroying data on computers. The virus may destroy what appear to be unimportant files until you attempt to use one of the programs or another feature of Windows, or it may erase all of your document files or corrupt the master boot record or complete registry file.

Viruses are spread through executable files (.exe) downloaded off the Internet or installed through a Flash drive. A virus can be disguised under the cloak of a Trojan, which is the carrier of the virus.

Worms replicate themselves, reaching over networks to multiple computers that are unprotected by firewalls. Worms come through email, through Trojans, and even via scripting code from users visiting unsavory Websites.

MOST POPULAR PROGRAMMING LANGUAGES TO LEARN IN 2023

Table of Contents

Once upon a time, the world of computer programming was a mysterious and exclusive place. Only a select handful of people were considered computer programmers with cutting-edge coding skills. Today, many IT jobs require a solid grasp of the top programming languages, and yes, we mean more than one.

If your plans to advance your career or change careers completely requires you to master a programming language, you might wonder which one to learn. After all, it will take time and money to learn the language, so you want to make the right choice.

When making your decision, you should bear several considerations in mind, like the difficulty level you're willing to tackle, the programming language knowledge you already possess that meshes with your existing coding skills, or your reasons for learning a top programming language.

Whether you want to develop a mobile application, get certification for programming knowledge, or learn new skills, you need to learn the right programming language. Below you'll learn about the best programming languages in demand among employers in 2023. You'll be briefed about the details of each language, its complexity, and how it is used.

What is a Programming Language?

A programming language is a way for programmers (developers) to communicate with computers. Programming languages consist of a set of rules that allows string values to be converted into various ways of generating machine code, or, in the case of visual programming languages, graphical elements.

Generally speaking, a program is a set of instructions written in a particular language (C, C++, Java, Python) to achieve a particular task.

What Are the Best Programming Languages to Learn in 2023?

What coding and programming language should i learn? JavaScript and Python, two of the most popular languages in the startup industry, are in high demand. Most startups use Python-based backend frameworks such as Django (Python), Flask (Python), and NodeJS (JavaScript). These languages are also considered to be the best programming languages to learn for beginners.

Below is a list of the most popular programming languages that will be in demand in 2023.

1. Javascript
2. Python
3. Go
4. Java
5. Kotlin
6. PHP
7. C#
8. Swift
9. R
10. Ruby
11. C and C++

12. Matlab

13. TypeScript

14. Scala

15. SQL

16. HTML

17. CSS

18. NoSQL

19. Rust

20. Perl

1. Javascript

JavaScript is a high-level programming language that is one of the core technologies of the World Wide Web. It is used as a client-side programming language by 97.8 percent of all websites. JavaScript was originally used only to develop web browsers, but they are now used for server-side website deployments and non-web browser applications as well.

Javascript was created in 1995 and was initially known as LiveScript. However, Java was a very popular language at that time, so it was advertised as a "younger brother" of Java. As it evolved over time, JavaScript became a fully independent language. Nowadays, JavaScript is often confused with Java, and although there are some similarities between them, the two languages are distinct.

2. Python

Python is one of the most popular programming languages today and is easy for beginners to learn because of its readability. It is a free, open-source programming language with extensive support modules and community development, easy integration with web services, user-friendly data structures, and GUI-based desktop applications. It is a popular programming language for machine learning and deep learning applications.

3. Go

Go was developed by Google in 2007 for APIs and web applications. Go has recently become one of the fastest-growing programming languages due to its simplicity, as well as its ability to handle multicore and networked systems and massive codebases.

Go, also known as Golang, was created to meet the needs of programmers working on large projects. It has gained popularity among many large IT companies thanks to its simple and modern structure and syntax familiarity. Companies using Go as their programming language include Google, Uber, Twitch, Dropbox, among many others. Go is also gaining in popularity among data scientists because of its agility and performance.

4. Java

Java is one of the most popular programming languages used today.

Owned by Oracle Corporation, this general-purpose programming language with its object-oriented structure has become a standard for applications that can be used regardless of platform (e.g., Mac, Windows, Android, iOS, etc.) because of its Write Once, Run Anywhere (WORA) capabilities. As a result, Java is recognized for its portability across platforms, from mainframe data centers to smartphones. Today there are more than 3 billion devices running applications built with Java.

Java is widely used in web and application development as well as big data. Java is also used on the backend of several popular websites, including Google, Amazon, Twitter, and YouTube. It is also extensively used in hundreds of applications. New Java frameworks like Spring, Struts, and Hibernate are also very popular. With millions of Java developers worldwide, there are hundreds of ways to learn Java. Also, Java programmers have an extensive online community and support each other to solve problems.

5. Kotlin

Kotlin is a general-purpose programming language originally developed and unveiled as Project Kotlin by JetBrains in 2011. The first version was officially released in 2016. It is interoperable with Java and supports functional programming languages.

Kotlin is used extensively for Android apps, web application, desktop application, and server-side application development. Kotlin was built to be better than Java, and people who use this language are convinced. Most of the Google applications are based on Kotlin. Some companies using Kotlin as their programming language include Coursera, Pinterest, PostMates among many others.

6. PHP

PHP is an open-source programming language created in 1990. Many web developers find it essential to learn PHP, as this language is used to build more than 80% of websites on the Internet, including notable sites like Facebook and Yahoo.

Programmers mainly use PHP mainly to write server-side scripts. But developers can also use this language to write command-line scripts, and programmers with high-level PHP coding skills can also use it to develop desktop applications.

PHP is considered a relatively easy language to learn for beginning developers. PHP professionals have access to several dedicated online communities, making it easy to get support and answers to questions.

7. C#

Developed by Microsoft, C# rose to fame in the 2000s for supporting the concepts of object-oriented programming. It is one of the most used programming languages for the .NET framework. Anders Hejlsberg, the creator of C#, says the language is more like C++ than Java.

8. Swift

A few years ago, Swift made the top 10 in the monthly TIOBE Index ranking of popular programming languages. Apple developed Swift in 2014 for Linux and Mac applications.

An open-source programming language that is easy to learn, Swift supports almost everything from the programming language Objective-C. Swift requires fewer coding skills compared with other programming languages, and it can be used with IBM

Swift Sandbox and IBM Bluemix. Swift is used in popular iOS apps like WordPress, Mozilla Firefox, SoundCloud, and even in the game Flappy Bird.

9. R

R is an open-source language that is essentially a different version of the S language. Much of the code that developers write for S runs on R without modification. Applications built in R are used for processing statistics, including linear and nonlinear modeling, calculation, testing, visualization, and analysis. Applications coded using R can interface with a number of databases and process both structured and unstructured data.

R has a moderate learning curve and is not as easy for beginners to pick up as some other languages in this article. However, like other open-source programming languages, R boasts an active online community of developers, which is always a plus when learning new coding skills.

10. Ruby

If you want to start with a language that is known for being relatively simple to learn, consider Ruby. Developed in the 1990s, it was designed to have a more human-friendly syntax while still being flexible from the standpoint of its object-oriented architecture that supports procedural and functional programming notation. A web-application framework that is implemented in Ruby is Ruby on Rails ("RoR"). Ruby developers tout it for being an easy language to write in and also for the relatively short learning time required. These attributes have led to a large community of Ruby developers and a growing interest in the language among beginning developers. The average salary for a Ruby developer is around $121,000 per year.

11. C and C++

C is probably the oldest and popular programming language and is the root of other programming languages such as C#, Java, and JavaScript. C++ is an enhanced version of C. Many developers today skip learning C on its own, while others think learning C first provides a valuable foundation for C++ development. Both languages are widely used in computer science and programming.

12. Matlab

Matlab is a proprietary programming language owned by MathWorks and originally released in the mid-1980s. It is built specifically for use by scientists and engineers. Programmers use Matlab to build machine learning and deep learning applications. Matlab-based programs enable users to analyze data, create algorithms, process images, and verify research.

Generally, Matlab is easier to learn than other programming languages on our list. MathWorks' website has an extensive section dedicated to answering questions about Matlab.

13. TypeScript

TypeScript is a newcomer to top programming language lists, but it's making headway. It was developed in 2012 by Microsoft and is a typed version of JavaScript that is well suited for large code bases. TypeScript is used to create JavaScript-based projects with typing in both client-side and server-side development, making useful for catching errors and preventing systemic issues.

14. Scala

Scala is a general-purpose, type-safe Java virtual machine language that combines the best oop and functional programming languages into one special high language. Scala is ideal for reducing and removing bugs in large, complex applications. It supports both object-oriented and functional programming.

Programmers can use Scala for any task that they normally would use Java for. Scala is a complex language, but that complexity gives it a lot of flexibility. Companies that use Scala include Netflix, Twitter, and the New York Times.

15. SQL

SQL is a standard database query language. It is used to access and manipulate data in databases. SQL is a declarative language that specifies the desired results, but not the steps to achieve those results. SQL is a powerful tool for accessing and manipulating data, and it is the world's most widely used database query language.

Benefits of SQL

- SQL is a standard database query language that enables users to manipulate and query data in a database quickly.
- SQL is widely used in many applications and environments, such as web applications, data warehouses, and e-commerce applications.
- SQL provides many benefits over other database query languages, such as improved performance, better data integrity, and more accessible data manipulation.

Cons of SQL

- If you are unfamiliar with programming or database concepts, SQL can be challenging to learn.
- SQL can be slow compared to other languages, mainly when working with large databases.
- And SQL is not well suited for certain types of tasks, such as complex mathematical calculations or machine learning.

16. HTML

HTML(HyperText Markup Language) is the standard language for creating web pages and applications. HTML is used to create web pages. You can use HTML to add images, links, and other types of content to your web page. HTML is a simple programming language; you don't need to know much about it to create a basic web page.

Images and other objects, such as interactive forms, can be embedded within the produced page using HTML structures. It enables the creation of structured documents by indicating structural semantics for text elements including as headings, paragraphs, lists, links, quotations, and other objects. HTML elements are delineated by tags, which are written in angle brackets.

Benefits of HTML

- Benefits of using HTML include creating well-structured, standards-compliant web pages that are easy to maintain and update.
- HTML is also easy to learn and is a great starting point for those new to web development.
- HTML is used to structure and present content on the web and is typically used alongside CSS and JavaScript.
- Additionally, HTML5 provides better multimedia and interactive content support, making it a powerful tool for creating engaging web experiences.
- HTML5 is the latest version and includes new features like video and audio elements, local storage, and 2D/3D graphics. HTML5 is designed to be more user-friendly and efficient than previous versions of HTML.

Cons of HTML

A few potential drawbacks exist to using HTML as a web development language.

- First, because HTML is a markup language, it is not as expressive as a programming language like JavaScript or PHP, which means that complex web applications or pages can be more challenging to develop in HTML.
- Additionally, HTML is not a very secure language, so web developers must carefully encode any user input to prevent security vulnerabilities properly.
- Finally, HTML can be somewhat challenging to learn for newcomers, as it has a lot of different

17. CSS

CSS (Cascading Style Sheets) is a style sheet language used to describe how a page that was produced in a markup language is presented. A style sheet, which is a set of rules for web browsers, can control an HTML or XML. All HTML tags, including the text in the document's body, headings, paragraphs, and other text elements, are styled using CSS. The display of grid components, table elements, and picture.

Benefits of CSS

- CSS is used to style all HTML tags, including the body of the document, headings, paragraphs, and other material. CSS can also be used to style how table components, grid elements, and images are displayed.

- Web developers use CSS to create responsive and accessible websites. CSS can make it easier for web developers to create websites that look good on all devices, including mobile phones and tablets.
- CSS can also help make websites more accessible to people with disabilities.
- CSS is easy to learn and use. Many tutorials and resources are available online, and anyone can start using CSS to style their web pages.

Con of CSS

- CSS can be challenging to debug. When there are errors in a CSS file, it can be difficult to track down the source of the problem.
- And it can be time-consuming to write. CSS files can be large and complex, and it can take a lot of time to create and maintain them.

Overall, the CSS is a powerful tool that can be used to style web documents. However, it is vital to know the potential drawbacks before using it.

18. NoSQL

NoSQL databases are non-relational databases designed to provide high performance and scalability. And NoSQL databases are often used in big data applications, where data is distributed across many nodes.

The four key categories of NoSQL databases are as follows:

- key-value stores,
- columnar stores,
- document stores,
- And graph databases.

Benefits of NoSQL

- NoSQL is a database system that does not use the traditional relational model.
- NoSQL databases are often used for big data applications that need to scale quickly.
- NoSQL databases can be faster and more scalable than relational databases.

Cons of NoSQL

- NoSQL databases are generally less mature than SQL databases and, as such, may lack some of the features and functionality that SQL databases offer.
- Additionally, because NoSQL databases are less standardized than SQL databases, it can be more challenging to find skilled personnel who can work with them.
- And NoSQL databases may be less compatible with existing applications and infrastructure than SQL databases.

19. Rust

Rust is a programming language designed to be safe, concurrent, and practical. It is a systems programming language that runs blazingly fast, prevents segfaults, and guarantees thread safety. Rust is also memory-efficient: it uses minimal memory, making it ideal for embedded systems.

Benefits of Rust

- Rust is a fast and efficient language used to create high-performance applications.
- Rust is also a safe and reliable language, which makes it perfect for developing mission-critical software.
- Additionally, Rust is easy to learn and use and has a great community of developers who are always willing to help.

Cons of Rust

While Rust has many features that make it an attractive language, there are some drawbacks to using it.

- There needs to be more support or documentation available for other languages because it is a new language, making it difficult to learn and use Rust.
- Additionally, Rust only supports some platforms, and it can be challenging to integrate with existing codebases.

20. Perl

Perl is an interpreted, high-level, general-purpose programming language. Although Perl is not officially an acronym, various backronyms exist, including "Practical Extraction and Report Language." Perl was originally developed by Larry Wall in 1987 as a general-purpose Unix scripting language to make report processing easier. Since then, it has undergone many changes and revisions.

Perl is widely regarded as the " Swiss Army knife" of programming languages because of its versatility and power. It is used for various tasks, including web development, network programming, system administration, and more.

Benefits of Perl

- Perl is a powerful programming language with many features and applications. It is widely used in system administration, web development, network programming, and many other fields.
- Perl is easy to learn, and its concise syntax makes it an excellent choice for beginners. It is also very versatile, allowing you to write programs in various styles.
- Perl has excellent support for many databases, making it a good choice for database-driven applications. It also has excellent support for graphics and multimedia, making it a good choice for media-rich applications.

Cons of Perl

Although Perl is an interesting and feature-rich programming language, it also has some cons.

- First of all, it is more challenging to learn than some other languages like Python, and it has a very steep learning curve and can confuse beginners.
- Additionally, Perl is not as widely used as other languages, so there is not as much support available.
- Finally, it can be pretty slow compared to some other languages.

MCQS

1. _______________ gets installed & stays hidden in your computer's memory. It stays involved to the specific type of files which it infects.

(A) Boot Sector Virus

(B) Direct Action Virus

(C) Polymorphic Virus

(D) Multipartite Virus

(E) None of these

Ans: B

2. Direct Action Virus is also known as ___________.

(A) Non-resident virus

(B) Boot Sector Virus

(C) Polymorphic Virus

(D) Multipartite Virus

(E) Space-filler Virus

Ans: A

3. The two broad categories of software are________.

(A) word processing and spreadsheet

(B) transaction and application

(C) Windows and Mac OS

(D) system and application

Correct Answer

(E) None of these

Ans: D

4. Which among the following is the Application software?

(A) Linux

(B) Unix

(C) Microsoft Power Point

(D) Macros

(E) Windows

Ans: C

5. A __________ is software, usually located at its own Web site, that lets a user specify search terms.

(A) Search engine

(B) Database engine

(C) Meta search engine

(D) Cluster

(E) None of these

Ans: A

6. The computer or server on the Internet is also known as:

(A) Host

(B) Address

(C) IP address

(D) URL address

(E) Web address

Ans: A

7. Which of the following is true about URL?

(A) It is a web browser

(B) It is a messenger

(C) It is a mail service

(D) It is a global address of documents and other resources on the World Wide Web.

(E) None of these

Ans: D

8. Voicemail, E-mail, Online service, the Internet and the WWW are all example of-

(A) Computer categories

(B) Connectivity

(C) Telecommuting

(D) Both (A) and (B)

(E) None of the above

Ans: C

9. Which of the following is a program that copies itself throughout a computer or network?

(A) Worms

(B) Trojans

(C) Viruses

(D) Rootkits

(E) None of above

Ans: C

10. Managed detection and response (MDR) is:

(A) a cybersecurity service that works on technology to perform threat hunting, monitoring, and response.

(B) a cybersecurity service that combines technology and human expertise to perform threat hunting, monitoring, and response.

(C) a cybersecurity service that separates technology and human expertise to perform threat hunting, monitoring, and response.

(D) a cybersecurity service where human expert works to perform threat hunting, monitoring, and response.

(E) All of above

Ans: B

11. Which is not a property of representation of knowledge?

(A) Representational Verification

(B) Representational Accuracy

(C) Inferential Adequacy

(D) Inferential Efficiency

(E) All of these

Answer: A

12. What is quantum computing?

(A) Quantum computing is the phenomenon of quantum mechanics in computation to solve certain problems.

(B) Quantum computing is an old technology used in computation.

(C) Quantum computing used in computation to solve certain physics problems only.

(D) Both (B) and (C)

(E) None of these

Answer : A

13. What is the difference between DBMS and RDBMS?

(A) A DBMS can be manipulated but an RDBMS cannot be

(B) A DBMS is a database of commercial type by an RDBMS is a data of engineers

(C) A DBMS cannot link up various files with one another whereas an RDBMS can

(D) (A) and (B) both

(E) None of these

Answer: C

14. What is part of a database that holds only one type of information?

(A) Report

(B) Field

(C) Record

(D) File

(E) None of these

Answer: B

15. In DBMS, all the data is stored at a ____________.

(A) Central

(B) Multiple

(C) RDBMS

(D) Both (A) and (B)

(E) None of these

Answer : A

16. The operation that does not involves clock cycles is _____________.

(A) Installation of a device

(B) Execute

(C) Fetch

(D) Decode

(E) None of these

Answer : A

17. Which of the following processor has a fixed length of instructions?

(A) CISC

(B) RISC

(C) EPIC

(D) Multi-core

(E) None of the above

Answer : B

18. Processor which is complex and expensive to produce _________.

(A) RISC

(B) EPIC

(C) CISC

(D) multi-core

(E) None of these

Answer : C

19. Flash Memory Cards are considered ___________, meaning that when you turn off the power, you will not lose your data.

(A) Temporary

(B) Peripherals

(C) Volatile

(D) non-volatile

(E) Both (A) and (B)

Answer : D

20. Ensuring that the essential peripheral devices are attached and operational is the __________ process.

(A) configuration

(B) CMOS

(C) POST

(D) ROM

(E) RAM

Answer : C

21. When you link data maintained in an Excel workbook to a word document, then what happens?

(A) The word document cannot be edit.

(B) The word document contains a reference to the original source application.

(C) The word document must contain a hyperlink.

(D) The word document contains a copy of the actual data.

(E) None of the above

Ans: B

22. Which command brings you to the first slide in your MS PowerPoint presentation?

(A) Next slide button

(B) Page up

(C) Ctrl + Home

(D) Ctrl +End

(E) Ctrl +Alt

Ans: C

23. Which of the following is true in relation to clip art?

(A) PowerPoint displays available pictures in the Clip Art Gallery.

(B) You can use a toolbar button or a palace holder.

(C) You can re-colour Clip Art.

(D) All of the above

(E) None of the above

Ans: D

24. What does LAN stand for?

(A) Local Area Nodes

(B) Large Area Network

(C) Large Area Nodes

(D) Local Area Network

(E) None of these

Ans: D

25. The ALU of a computer responds to the commands coming from ________.

(A) Primary memory

(B) Control section

(C) External memory

(D) Cache memory

(E) None of these

Ans: B

26. Which of the following languages is more suited to a structured program?

(A) PL/1

(B) FORTRAN

(C) BASIC

(D) PASCAL

(E) None of the above

Ans: D

27. A set of computer programs that helps a computer monitor itself and function more efficiently is a/an __________.

(A) Java

(B) system software

(C) DBMS

(D) application software

(E) HTML

Ans: B

28. A _____ is a device that not only provides surge protection but also furnishes your computer with battery backup power during a power outage.

(A) Surge strip

(B) USB

(C) UPS

(D) Battery strip

(E) Both (A) and (B)

Ans: C

29. The period of ________ generation was 1952-1964.

(A) 1st

(B) 2nd

(C) 5th

(D) 4th

(E) 3rd

Ans: B

30. Which was the first electronic digital programmable computing device?

(A) Analytical Engine

(B) Difference Engine

(C) Colossus

(D) ENIAC

(E) None of the above

Ans: C

31. In MS Word when Ctrl + Shift with any of the arrow keys is used, it will __________.

(A) Select a block of text

(B) Deletes something

(C) Paste something

(D) (A) and (B) both

(E) None of these

Answer: A

32. F1 key is used for ___________.

(A) Help

(B) Print

(C) View

(D) Save

(E) None of these

Answer : A

33. What problem is solved by Dijkstra's banker's algorithm?

(A) mutual exclusion

(B) deadlock recovery

(C) deadlock avoidance

(D) cache coherence

(E) None of the above

Answer: C

34. When the process issues an I/O request __________.

(A) It is placed in an I/O queue

(B) It is placed in a waiting queue

(C) It is placed in the ready queue

(D) It is placed in the Job queue

(E) None of the above

Answer: A

35. The processes that are residing in main memory and are ready and waiting to execute are kept on a list called _____________.

(A) job queue

(B) ready queue

(C) execution queue

(D) process queue

(E) None of the above

Answer : B

36. What is backup?

(A) Adding more components to your network

(B) Protecting data by copying it from the original source to a different destination

(C) Filtering old data from the new data

(D) (A) and (B) both

(E) All of the above

Answer : B

37. MODEM word is made from:

(A) Modulation, Demodulation

(B) Modulation, Rough modulation

(C) Modulation, Defination

(D) (A) and (B) both

(E) All of above

Answer : A

38. A cookie _______.

(A) Stores information about the user's web activity

(B) Stores software developed by the user

(C) Stores the password of the user

(D) Stores the commands used by the user

(E) Stores lost data

Answer : A

39. A _______ module is a device that converts spoken words into information that the computer can recognize and process.

(A) Microphone

(B) Voice recognition

(C) Optical Scanner

(D) Video Graphic adapter

(E) None of these

Answer : B

40. The place where programs, files and data are stored in the computer is called?

(A) CPU

(B) Hard Disk

(C) RAM

(D) Motherboard

(E) None of these

Answer : B

41. Which of the below-mentioned reasons do not satisfy the reason why people create a computer virus?

(A) Research purpose

(B) Pranks

(C) Identity theft

(D) Protection

(E) Steal data

Ans: D

42. Code Red is a type of ________.

(A) Antivirus Program

(B) photo editing software

(C) computer virus

(D) video editing software

(E) None of these

Ans: C

43. Reusable optical storage will typically have the acronym:

(A) CD

(B) RD

(C) DVD

(D) ROM

(E) None of these

Ans: E

44. A program that provides software interface to hardware devices is called __________.

(A) System Software

(B) Application Software

(C) Device Drivers

(D) Microchip

(E) All of the Above

Ans: C

45. Which of the following is a function of the control unit?

(A) Read instructions

(B) Execute instructions

(C) Interpret instructions

(D) Direct operations

(E) None of these

Ans: D

46. World Wide Web pages can be described as multimedia pages. This means that the pages may contain.

(A) Text, pictures, sound

(B) Text and pictures only

(C) Video clips, text, pictures

(D) Video clips, sound

(E) All of the above

Ans: E

47. In HTTPS, 'S' is stands for:

(A) Simple

(B) Secured

(C) Server

(D) Speed

(E) None of these

Ans: B

48. The size of an IP address in IPv6 is _________.

(A) 32 bits

(B) 64 bits

(C) 128 bits

(D) 265 bits

(E) 320 bits

Ans: C

49. Which malware enable administrative control, allowing an attacker to do almost anything on an infected computer?

(A) Rootkits

(B) RATs

(C) Botnets

(D) Worms

(E) All of above

Ans: B

50. What is true regarding Trojans?

(A) Trojans will conduct whatever action they have been programmed to carry out.

(B) "Trojan" alludes to the mythological story of Greek soldiers hidden inside a wooden horse that was given to the enemy city of Troy.

(C) Trojans do not replicate or reproduce through infection.

(D) Trojan horse is the name given to a computer virus.

(E) All of these

Ans: E

51. What is full form ANSI?

(A) American Nation Standard Instruction Codes

(B) American National Standards Institute

(C) Asian National Standard Instruction Codes

(D) Asian Nations Standard Instruction Codes

(E) None of these

Answer: B

52. What is the full form of BPS?

(A) Bytes Per Second

(B) Bits Per Second

(C) Bytes Pro Second

(D) Bits Per Secure

(E) None of these

Answer : B

53. In a relational database, tables are logically linked to each other by a:

(A) Key

(B) Hyperlink

(C) Field type

(D) Field size

(E) Linker

Answer: A

54. What field type is best to store serial numbers?

(A) Number

(B) AutoNumber

(C) Text

(D) Memo

(E) None of these

Answer: B

55. Which of the following is not a component of relational database?

(A) Entity

(B) Attribute

(C) Table

(D) Hierarchy

(E) All of the above

Answer : D

56. A device similar to a flash drive ______________.

(A) Memory card

(B) Compact drive

(C) Compact disk

(D) Memory disk

(E) None of these

Answer : A

57. Which of the following is not a magnetic disk?

(A) Floppy

(B) Winchester

(C) Zip

(D) FLASH

(E) None of the above

Answer : D

58. Sending data from one place to another, by physical or electronic means is:

(A) E-mail

(B) Internet

(C) Data transmission

(D) Distributed processing

(E) None of the above

Answer : C

59. PCs are considered fourth generation and contain_____.

(A) Information

(B) Data

(C) Vacuum tubes

(D) Very Large Scale Integrated (VLSI) circuits

(E) None of these

Answer : D

60. Which of the following format you can decide to apply or not in the auto format dialog box?

(A) Number format

(B) Border format

(C) Font format

(D) Table format

(E) All of the above

Answer : D

61. How can you remove borders applied in cells?

(A) Choose None on Border tab of Format cells

(B) Open the list on Border tool in Format Cell toolbar then choose the first tool (none)

(C) The selected cells will change to the new formatting style

(D) Select the desired formatting option

(E) None of the above

Ans: C

62. The ability to combine name and addresses with a standard document is called _________.

(A) document formatting

(B) database management

(C) mail merge

(D) form letters

(E) None of these

Ans: C

63. The keystrokes Ctrl + I is used to:

(A) Increase font size

(B) Inserts a line break

(C) Applies italic format to selected text

(D) Indicate the text should be bold

(E) None of these

Ans: C

64. Move to the next option or option group use ______.

(A) Alt+tab

(B) Ctrl+tab

(C) Tab

(D) Ctrl+right arrow

(E) None of these

Ans: C

65. Who has developed the Automatically Programmable Tool (APT)?

(A) Gary Kildall

(B) Jonathan Fletcher

(C) Ralph H Baer

(D) Douglas T Ross

(E) None of these

Ans: D

66. A function declared as the "friend" function can always access the data in _______.

(A) The private part of its class

(B) The part declared as public of its class

(C) Class of which it is the member

(D) (A) and (B) both

(E) None of these

Ans: C

67. Source program is compiled to an intermediate form called ___________.

(A) Byte Code

(B) Smart code

(C) Executable code

(D) Machine code

(E) None of these

Ans: A

68. Which language used in second Generation computers?

(A) Machine language

(B) Assembly language

(C) High level language

(D) BASIC

(E) None of the above

Ans: C

69. Which is the first programmable analog computer?

(A) South-Pointing Chariot

(B) Planisphere

(C) Castle Clock

(D) Astrolabe

(E) None of the above

Ans: C

70. What type of scheduling is round-robin scheduling?

(A) Linear data scheduling

(B) Non-linear data scheduling

(C) Preemptive scheduling

(D) Non-preemptive scheduling

(E) None of the above

Ans: C

71. The characteristic of Feed back queue is-

(A) Are very easy to implement

(B) Dispatch tasks according to execution characteristics

(C) Are used to favor real-time tasks

(D) Require manual intervention to implement properly

(E) None of the above

Answer: B

72. In which addressing mode the operand is given explicitly in the instruction?

(A) Absolute mode

(B) Immediate mode

(C) Indirect mode

(D) Index mode

(E) None of the above

Answer : B

73. The situation wherein the data of operands are not available is called _________.

(A) Stock

(B) Deadlock

(C) Data hazard

(D) Structural hazard

(E) Stock hazard

Answer: C

74. The divide and conquer approach is known for:

(A) Sequential algorithm development

(B) Parallel algorithm develpoment

(C) Task defined algorithm

(D) Non defined Algorithm

(E) Single algorithm develpoment

Answer: A

75. Frames from one LAN can be transmitted to another LAN via the device:

(A) Router

(B) Bridge

(C) Repeater

(D) Modem

(E) None of these

Answer : B

76. The slowest haulage speeds are among the following:

(A) Twisted-pair cabling

(B) Coaxial wire

(C) Fiber optic cable

(D) Microwave

(E) None of these

Answer : A

77. What do we call a network whose elements may be separated by some distance, it usually involves two or more small networks and dedicated high speed telephone lines?

(A) URL

(B) LAN

(C) WAN

(D) WWW

(E) MAN

Answer : C

78. A projector is an ______ device that can take images generated by a computer and reproduce them on a large, flat surface.

(A) input

(B) output

(C) input and output

(D) monitor input

(E) None of these

Answer : B

79. The OCR stands for?

(A) Outsized Character Reader

(B) Optical Character Reader

C) Operational Character Reader

(D) Only Character Reader

(E) None of these

Answer : B

80. ______________ is also known as cavity virus.

(A) Non-resident virus

(B) Overwrite Virus

(C) Polymorphic Virus

(D) Space-filler Virus

(E) Multipartite virus

Answer : D

81. The virus that spread in application software is called as __________.

(A) Boot virus

(B) Macro virus

(C) File virus

(D) Anti virus

(E) All of the above

Ans: B

82. A Web site's main page is called its______________.

(A) Home Page

(B) Browser Page

(C) Search Page

(D) Bookmark

(E) All of the above

Ans: A

83. The Internet Protocol (IP) ______________.

(A) Handles software computer addresses

(B) Finds the quickest route between two computers

(C) Ensures that connections are maintained between computers

(D) Both (A) and (B)

(E) None of the above

Ans: A

84. _____ is the term used to refer to the process of two modems establishing communications with each other.

(A) Interacting

(B) Handshaking

(C) Connecting

(D) Linking

(E) Pinging

Ans: B

85. Missing slot covers on a computer can cause?

(A) Overheat

(B) Power surges

(C) EMI

(D) The incomplete path for ESD

(E) None of the above

Ans: A

86. Which among the following is not a peripheral hardware device in a computer system?

(A) Keyboard

(B) Optical Drive

(C) HDD

(D) Printer

(E) None of the above

Ans: C

87. Malware is a short form of ____________.

(A) malicious hardware

(B) malicious software

(C) designed to cause damage to a stand-alone computer

(D) Both (A) and (B)

(E) Both (B) and (C)

Ans: E

88. Which malware has short for "robot network"?

(A) Ronets

(B) Botnets

(C) Botwork

(D) Rowork

(E) None of these

Ans: B

89. What is the full form of IP?

(A) Internal Protocol

(B) Internet Protocol

(C) Interior Protocol

(D) All of the above

(E) None of these

Ans: B

90. What is the full form of UTP?

(A) Unshielded Twisted Pair

(B) Universal Transmission Path

(C) User Time Precision

(D) Unified Transmission Protocol

(E) None of these

Ans: A

91. Indexes created from a sequential set of primary keys are referred to as ___.

(A) Indexed file organization

(B) Sequential file

(C) Index sequential

(D) All of the above

(E) None of these

Answer: C

92. The purpose of the primary key in a database is to_____.

(A) unlock the database

(B) a relationship between two tables

(C) uniquely identify a record

(D) establish constraints on database operations.

(E) None of these

Answer : B

93. Which one of the following keywords are used to find out the number of values in a column?

(A) TOTAL

(B) COUNT

(C) SUM

(D) ADD

(E) None of the above

Answer: B

94. Storage which stores or retains data after power off is called-

(A) Volatile storage

(B) Non- volatile storage

(C) Sequential storage

(D) Direct storage

(E) None of the above

Answer: B

95. Which of the following will you require to hear music on your computer?

(A) Video Card

(B) Sound Card

(C) Mouse

(D) Joy Stick

(E) All of the above

Answer : B

96. Which device consists of electronic circuits that interpret and execute program instructions?

(A) Central processing unit

(B) Input

(C) Output

(D) Pointer

(E) Scanner

Answer : A

97. What function displays row data in a column or column data in a row?

(A) Hyperlink

(B) Index

(C) Transpose

(D) Rows

(E) Cells

Answer : B

98. Which of the following menus has a background in PowerPoint 2003?

(A) Format

(B) View

(C) Insert

(D) Slide show

(E) None of these

Answer : C

99. What is the maximum number of columns in a worksheet of Excel 2007?

(A) 1024

(B) 2048

(C) 256

(D) 3072

(E) None of these

Answer : E

100. Quantum computing is relatively ___________ than classical computing.

(A) Slower

(B) Faster

(C) Average

(D) Smaller

(E) None of these

Answer : B

www.ingramcontent.com/pod-product-compliance
Ingram Content Group UK Ltd.
Pitfield, Milton Keynes, MK11 3LW, UK
UKHW061703190726
13853UKWH00008B/2381

9 789355 566010